Isaac Butts

Protection and Free Trade

An inquiry whether protective duties can benefit the interests of a country in the aggregate - including an examination into the nature of value, and the agency of the natural forces in producing it

Isaac Butts

Protection and Free Trade

An inquiry whether protective duties can benefit the interests of a country in the aggregate - including an examination into the nature of value, and the agency of the natural forces in producing it

ISBN/EAN: 9783337228101

Printed in Europe, USA, Canada, Australia, Japan

Cover: Foto ©Suzi / pixelio.de

More available books at **www.hansebooks.com**

PROTECTION

AND

FREE TRADE:

AN INQUIRY WHETHER PROTECTIVE DUTIES CAN BENEFIT THE INTERESTS OF A COUNTRY IN THE AGGREGATE; INCLUDING AN EXAMINATION INTO THE NATURE OF VALUE, AND THE AGENCY OF THE NATURAL FORCES IN PRODUCING IT.

BY

ISAAC BUTTS.

NEW YORK:
G. P. PUTNAM'S SONS,
FOURTH AVE & TWENTY-THIRD STREET.
1875.

EDITOR'S PREFACE.

The posthumous appearance of this work requires a word of explanation. The author entrusted its publication to the writer during an illness which terminated fatally on the twentieth of November, 1874. It was nearly ready for the press, and is printed as he left it, except that a brief "conclusion," found in an unfinished state, and containing nothing essential to the argument, is omitted.

Mr. Butts was in his 59th year at the time of his decease. He was born in Dutchess County, N. Y., in 1816, and removed with his parents, in early life, to the vicinity of Rochester.

The greater part of the active life of Mr. Butts was devoted to journalism. His connection with the press began in 1844. For nearly twenty years he occupied a prominent and influential position as Editor-in-chief of one of the leading daily newspapers in the interior of the State of New York. He became widely known as an able political writer, and an advocate of democratic principles of government.

A temporary suspension of his editorial labors occurred between 1848 and 1850, and his attention was turned at this early period to the electric telegraph, the practical use of which, in the United States, dates from 1844. Among the organizations which have grown out of this invention, none have equalled, in magnitude and importance of interests, The Western Union Telegraph Company. This enterprise originated in Rochester. The first step was the formation of a company in 1850, for the use of House's Printing Telegraph, to which the subject of our sketch was a contributor. This was merged in 1851 in "The New York and Mississippi Valley Printing Telegraph Company," in which he was also interested. This corporate name was changed in 1856 to the one given above. Mr. Butts became one of the first directors of the Western Union Company, was long associated with its management, and took an active part in the various measures of extension and consolidation which made it the greatest telegraph company in the world.

Having been highly successful in business, he retired in 1864 from journalism to private life, and the care of an estate, which was identified with the prosperity of the city of his residence. Municipal policy thus forced itself upon his attention; and his pen was often and ably used in the discussion of principles and measures involved in the government of municipalities.

The present volume will testify for how long a period the subject of political economy had occupied his thoughts. In his retirement it became his favorite study; and was regarded by him as second in importance to no other. Besides occasional publications on this subject, he prepared the present treatise on Protection, Value, etc., as an argument for free trade, based upon principles rather than upon statistical premises.

It would be difficult to do justice in few words to the intellectual character of Mr. Butts. As a journalist he exhibited a marked individuality, and the sagacity of the most successful political writers. His method was logical, and was used with great thoroughness and force. In view of his unquestioned ability, and long-continued services as an editor, he must be ranked with the foremost men of his profession.

But among his characteristics, none are more pleasing to remember than those relating to his private and social life. Of unpretending manners, and pure tastes, he was highly esteemed as a companion, and a friend: while his affection for his family manifested itself as a ruling passion.

As the public life of Mr. Butts secured to him

many personal acquaintances, who, with a large circle of friends, may take an interest in his last literary work, it has been deemed proper to add a portrait, and this brief biographical sketch, as a memorial tribute to the author.

W. W. É.

ROCHESTER, N. Y.,
January, 1875.

CONTENTS.

	PAGE.
Editor's Preface	5
Author's Preface	11
On Protection as a National Policy	17
On Value	27
Property in Land	68
The Relation of Nature's Forces and Materials to Value, further considered	83
Re-statement and Application of Principles	111
Natural Indications as to the Employment of Capital and Labor	116
Claims of Protectionism	122
Diversification of Industry	123
Protectionism works a Diminution of Natural and General Wealth	133
Countervailing Duties	134
Transportation considered in its Economical Aspects	137
The "Natural Places" for Manufacturing Machinery	146
The Conversion of Idlers into Producers	149
Protectionism and Commerce	150
Adam Smith and Say on Internal and Foreign Commerce	155
Commerce	161
Sundry other Protectionist Arguments and Positions, briefly stated	166
The Time Plea	
Protection against Cheap Foreign Labor	170
A Revenue Tariff	179
APPENDIX A. A Paper read before the Rochester Free Trade League	183
APPENDIX B. Extracts from Bastiat's Works	188

PREFACE.

It is a well-known fact, that the combustion of a given quantity of carbon will produce a definite quantity of heat, and that such quantity cannot be increased by varying the rate or mode of combustion.

Given then, the quantity of carbon, and science can determine the precise quantity of heat (as also of power) which its combustion will generate — a quantity which no contrivance, however ingenious, can enable the manipulator to surpass.

The method I have adopted in the following pages and applied to a question of political economy, bears some analogy to the method by which the greatest possible quantity of heat obtainable would be determined, the quantity of carbon being given. But I wish it distinctly understood that attention is invited to the analogy referred to, simply to enable the reader the more readily to comprehend the nature of my argument, and that it is designed to form no part of the argument itself.

I have endeavored to show what are the necessary elements of value, and what the conditions most favorable to the active co-operation of these elements in the production of values. Assuming that this part of my work has been successfully performed, I have pointed out that the quantity of these elements cannot be increased by means of "protection" so called, and that any interference by the government of sufficient potency to change the natural order of industries—by inducing capital and labor to transfer themselves from one industry to another—must inevitably violate the conditions of the largest possible production of values, and consequently diminish the aggregate which it avowedly aims to increase.

The method here briefly outlined, rendered it necessary to consider very carefully what is the true nature of value itself. And to this inquiry I have accordingly devoted more space than to any other which is subordinate to the main question under consideration.

"Political Economy," says Prof. Perry, "is the science of value and of nothing else." Value "is not an attribute of any one thing, but a relation subsisting between two things," says the same author. Frederic Bastiat was the first to define value as "a relation," and his definition has been very generally adopted by writers on political economy. To no man perhaps does political economy owe the recognition of its just claims as a science, so much as to him. And it seems to me probable that the authority of his great name may have prevented the reexamination into the real nature of value, which would have taken place by other thinkers on the subject, had he not so speciously argued and so positively asserted that value is simply and only a relation. He believed he had made a discovery of great value to science when he reached the conclusion that "value is a relation" and nothing more, and he exerts all his great powers of argument and illustration to establish the correctness of his new definition. That the mind naturally defers to eminent authority and accepts its conclusions in respect to questions requiring much thought for their independent solution, is well known to every student of scientific subjects. Thus, when value came up as a collateral question in the preparation of an article on Capital and Labor, published in the North American Review, January, 1873, I adopted the new definition of value without stopping to consider it with a view to determining for myself whether or not it is strictly accurate. But when it became necessary in preparing this work to analyze value, and to examine critically into its constitution, I was forced to the conclusion that value is something else than a simple "relation" or "external ratio," and that the new definition is therefore inaccurate and defective. The reasons for that conclusion—the substance of which is repeated in several chapters—will be found in the proper place.

Another position to which Bastiat attributes the greatest possible importance is, that the materials and forces which nature supplies, even when appropriated by man as private property, do not possess value themselves and cannot concur or co-operate in the creation of value; but that on the contrary they or the results of their action, are and will always remain gratuitous "throughout all human transactions." This he says is the ruling idea or "dominant thought" of his work.

It is quite needless to say to those who have read Bastiat's economical writings—unfortunately a very small portion of our people—that he invests his favorite conception with a good degree of plausibility. Yet I apprehend that it is unsound and that its abandonment would tend greatly to simplify many problems which have long perplexed economists. According to the theory herein proposed, the soundness of Bastiat's position is necessarily involved in every question relating to production; and I have therefore discussed it under various heads and at considerable length.

It will be observed that I have made no use of statistics, for reasons very briefly mentioned. It must not hence be inferred that I place too low an estimate on the value of statistics to the political economist and the statesman. Much reflection on this subject has led me to the conclusion that statistics are utterly incompetent to settle the question whether or not a scale of duties can be devised that would prove beneficial to the interests of a country considered in the aggregate. The very fact that the question has been earnestly argued from statistical premises, for more than one hundred and fifty years without decisive results, would seem to afford a strong presumption that the statistical method is altogether inadequate to its solution.

I have placed in the Appendix (marked A.) a paper prepared by me and read before a few gentlemen comprising the "Rochester Free Trade League," in January, 1851, in which will be found a brief outline of the argument more fully presented in the following pages. I have also placed in the Appendix (marked B.) several articles from Bastiat's Works, enforcing and illustrating his dominant idea that the materials and forces of nature are always free, and never constitute an element of value in any form whatever.

ON PROTECTION AS A NATIONAL POLICY.

Does a protective tariff, so called, benefit a country, as a whole?

That is, including all lawful interests and industrial enterprises of a country, in the comparison, would they, on the average, prosper better under a high tariff or under a free-trade policy?

This question covers all the debatable ground between the American protectionists and the free-traders. H. C. Carey, the highest protectionist authority in the United States, denounces indirect taxation by means of tariffs for revenue, in the severest terms he can employ. He places the inequitable distribution of wealth, caused by a revenue tariff, on a level with the "distribution" caused by pocket-picking; indeed, he describes the operation of such a tariff as pocket-picking by public authority. He proceeds to say:

"Tariffs, *for revenue*, should have no existence. Interferences with trade are to be tolerated only as measures of self-protection."*

A pupil of Carey's, who adopts all his arguments, theories and conclusions, but who excels his master in simplicity and force of expression, says:

* H. C. Carey's "Present, Past and Future," p. 472.

"If there is any valid reason for giving *any* degree of protection, it must be for the purpose of *cheapening production*, not for the purpose of enabling a *favored class* of producers to continue a business which would otherwise be unprofitable, by making up their losses out of the pockets of the consumers." *

The evils incident to protection are here distinctly admitted; but the admission is accompanied by the allegation that these incidental evils are more than counterbalanced by the benefits which protection confers upon society in the aggregate—upon the people, as a whole, not simply upon " a favored class of producers." It is, hence, clear that the question, " Does a protective tariff benefit the country, as a whole?" presents the issue fairly and in very simple terms.

That question alone it is proposed to consider. It is very evident that this question can never be effectually settled by means of arguments based upon statistics. Two authors, who have published large volumes, filled with statistics, one for the purpose of proving that protection does benefit the country as a whole, the other that it does not, have candidly or inadvertently confessed that statistics may be used on either side with equal effect.†

---

* E. Peshine Smith's "Political Economy," p. 268.

† A person employed in the preparation of government statistics, inquired, on being asked to prepare some tables, what was the policy

Yet it is unquestionable that statistics have most important and legitimate uses in respect to the industrial and commercial affairs of every nation. Nor can there be any question that they might be used to demonstrate the net effect of any given principle, measure or policy applied anew, upon the general prosperity of a country, taking all its interests into the account, were it possible to ascertain and verify *all the facts* which are indispensable to a full and exact statement of the benefits and injuries accruing to different parties and industries, which always result from governmental interference with the business affairs of the people. But it would seem that this is, and must ever remain, absolutely impossible. Suppose, for instance, heavy duties are imposed upon an article hitherto largely imported, and as a consequence capital and labor are diverted from other pursuits to the production of the "protected" commodity in enormous quantities—for which there is a ready sale in the absence of foreign competition. Suppose, further, that the first ten years of "protection" shows an excess in the production of the favored commodity to the extent of say $10,000,000,

to be proved. " Why," said the other, " Could you prove both sides ? " " Equally well," said he. [H.C.Carey's " Harmony of Interests," p. 4.]

This world has all sorts of facts in it, and the man who searches with a fixed idea in his head, will always find facts to fit that idea. [W. M. Grosvenor's " Does Protection Protect?" p. 9.]

as compared with that of the previous decade; that flourishing villages have sprung up around the manufacturing centres, furnishing an excellent "home market" to the farmers of the respective neighborhoods; and that real estate in these several localities has accordingly risen rapidly in value. The benefits of "protection," here indicated, taking the prices and products of the preceding ten years as the basis of comparison, could be ascertained with a tolerable degree of accuracy; and they would furnish statistics of great interest as well as arguments of great force to the particular class who had profited by state interference.

But these statistics would not prove that "protection" had benefited the country, as a whole— that the sum of its benefits had exceeded the sum of its injuries.

In order to decide the main question by means of statistics, it would still be necessary to ascertain, among other things, how much of the increased products is due to state interference only, and how much to other causes; how much more the favored products have cost the consumers in consequence of "protection;" how much capital and labor have been forced to abandon other industries by the reflected burdens of the protective policy; how much net gain they have realized from their new employment; how much, if any, such net gain exceeds what would have been the net gain of the same labor and capital had not state interference made their former employments unprofitable; and generally, to what extent the protective policy has injuriously affected the country by substituting artificial regulation of its industries for the genial rule of the natural laws.

Let us take the iron manufacture of America to illustrate the difficulty of obtaining and verifying the facts indispensable to an accurate and reliable comparison of the effects of the opposing policies on the prosperity of the country, as a whole. Iron has been made in this country more than two hundred years; and according to highly respectable authority "the production of iron has gone right on increasing in every decade of our history as a nation."* In colonial times, instead of receiving the protection of the mother country, it had to encounter its frowns. Who can tell how much more rapidly and at what cost to other industries it would have grown under favoring imperial auspices? Not till 1815—forty years after our independence, and after its successful production for more than one hundred and fifty years without protection—a duty of one dollar a ton was levied on pig iron. These facts prove one thing, and that by no means an unimportant one,—

* "N. Y. Financier," October 19, 1872.

that in the absence of discriminating legislative favor, the manufacture of iron can not only exist but prosper in a new country where land is fertile and cheap; but it must be admitted that they do not prove that the aggregate interests of the country might not have been promoted by a high tariff on iron. In regard to this vital question the facts referred to possess no significance whatever. Starting anew from 1816, since which time iron has been constantly though in varying degrees protected by federal legislation, its production has increased much more rapidly than it did prior to that date. But there can be no doubt whatever that had no duty been imposed on iron, considering the enormous development of the railroad system which has distinguished the last forty years, together with the constantly growing demand for iron for other purposes, there would have been a very large increase in its production in this country.

Still, however, the excess of the aggregate quantity of iron produced since the inauguration of the protective policy in 1816, over the quantity which *would have been* produced under a strict free trade policy, cannot, in the nature of things, ever be accurately or even approximately ascertained. And if it is impossible to ascertain this excess—one of the simplest elements of the grand problem—it would seem that all attempts to demonstrate by the selection and arrangement of statistics, that one or the other of the two antagonistic policies would best promote the interests of the country, *as a whole*, must necessarily and utterly fail.

Yet the fact that one or the other of these rival policies is the best for the country—including all lawful interests in the comparison—will not be questioned; and if for one country, the proposition, as will be shown hereafter, must be equally true of every other country, regardless of the fact that any particular country or countries may adhere to the opposite policy. The grand question, as already stated, is *which of the two?* And what is wanted is, not statistical or other arguments which simply confirm existing opinions and intensify old prejudices—thus fortifying error on whichever side it lies, and always rendering the ultimate acceptance of THE TRUTH more difficult as well as more remote; but, arguments from which every uncertain and doubtful element shall have been eliminated and whose conclusions shall possess all the force of demonstration. This want it is the proper function of argument and reason to supply; and the earnest and sincere efforts of the humblest devotee of science to supply it, cannot but be regarded as praiseworthy, even though they fall short of complete success.

A very brief outline of the plan adopted for this paper may properly be given in advance. The presence of "the universal motor, self-interest," is assumed here, as in every discussion of economical questions. It will then be my purpose to show—

1st. That there are two, and but two elements or factors, which are necessary to the production of wealth or the creation of new values, viz: Human labor and the natural forces, including in the latter term matter in its natural conditions.

2d. That the natural forces offer to labor widely different terms of co-operation in different countries and even in different parts of the same country; in virtue of which fact the same labor guided by like intelligence and having like advantages of capital in either case, will, under certain circumstances, produce a greater value than it will under certain other circumstances.

3d. That the sum of labor and of natural forces respectively in any country at any specific time, being given, though (especially the latter) not determinable quantities; and labor, under such direction as the intelligence of the country is capable of supplying, always seeking the most advantageous co-operation with the natural forces: therefore any legislation which, by bounties or other means, constrains labor, i. e., *the labor* of the country *as a whole,* to forego the more advantageous for a less advantageous co-operation of the natural forces, necessarily diminishes the efficiency of one of the elements or factors of production, and thereby lessens the aggregate of values produced, and injures the general prosperity of the country.

An examination of any given product possessing value would show to the ordinary observer that in its production capital and labor had co-operated with the natural forces. But such an examination and its results would not show what are the necessary or indispensable elements in the production of values; for here we have capital or *value itself* enumerated as one of the elements of the valuable product to be analyzed. If the capital or product here referred to as an element possessing value which entered into the composition of the "given product" subjected to examination, be *itself* examined, it will be found to be formed of the same elements as the first, viz.: pre-existing values or products, labor and natural forces. Should the same process be carried back *far enough,* it would be found that "in the beginning" of man's history, to whatever date it may be assigned, there was no wealth, no material object possessing value; and that he was obliged to satisfy his wants by utilizing, as best he could, the crude materials which nature had placed at his disposal. Whether his first stock of food was the fruit of the earth or the flesh of animals, is immaterial; it is certain that he or some successor was able, in a given time, to take or produce more food than was absolutely necessary for his sustenance for the time given, and that, during the period for which his surplus food sufficed him, he supplied himself with some better means than his bare hands afforded to procure his subsistence and satisfy his increasing wants. Such, in substance, must have been the process by which the first "wealth" or things of value were produced. And the rude contrivance for trapping game, or catching fish, which the first inventor wrought out with his hands from the raw materials furnished by nature, according to an ideal model of his own conception, was, in a scientific sense, just as truly capital, and, by proper analysis, it will be found to contain precisely the same simple elements, as capital invested in the complicated and gigantic machinery of the present time. Moreover, it is tolerably safe, though, for the purposes of my argument, quite unnecessary, to assume, that never in the unwritten history of our race, since our remote ancestor's accumulated stock of provisions enabled him to turn his mental and physical powers to producing his first "machine," has the world been entirely destitute of capital to facilitate the operations of human industry:

ON VALUE.

What is value? Bastiat describes it as the relation existing between two services exchanged; the "services" generally being represented by or embodied in commodities or things which, though the product of labor, and necessary for the satisfaction of human wants, do not themselves "possess value," excepting in a figurative sense—value itself being only a relation. Political economists, since the time of Bastiat, have very generally accepted his definition as correct. In their hands value, although the acknowledged basis of a most important science, ceases to be a tangible thing, or a quality, property or attribute of any tangible or conceivable thing. It is simply "a ratio—an external relation,"* and hence the idea of "intrinsic value" is an absurdity. The term itself, according to the writer just quoted, is a fruitful source of confusion and error, and it should be proscribed as an obstacle to progress in economical science. Yet it is worthy of note here, that the same author had occasion to use it on subsequent pages; and it will be evident on reading the context

* McLeod's "Theory of Banking," Vol. I. p. 50.

that he would have found it extremely difficult to select any other term to convey his meaning with equal clearness. Certainly no term or phrase harmonizing with the idea that "value is a ratio—an external relation"—would have answered his purpose.

Now, all values, considered with reference to other values, must be relative. But assuming that value is simply *a relation*, the question arises—a relation to, with or between what? To say it is a relation to, or with *other relations*, not otherwise defined or definable, would be unsatisfactory. The existence of relations necessarily implies the existence of *other things* to which such relations refer; and, in this case, these things are *values*—however defined. It seems to me that in respect to every material object, possessing exchangeable value, value may be briefly defined as any property or quality attaching to or inherent in such object, which renders it desirable and enables it to satisfy our wants. Whatever that property or quality may be, it must be the result of *effort* or *labor*, or be unobtainable by the person desiring it, without effort or labor; since otherwise it would possess no purchasing power or exchangeable value. And it is that property or quality— subject as it is to almost infinite variation—which invests a given material object in which it inheres or to which it attaches, with what is not inappropriately spoken of as "intrinsic value." It appears perfectly clear to me that the thing termed "intrinsic value" is an undeniable entity; and that scientific progress would not be promoted either by ignoring its existence or discarding the title by which it is ordinarily known.

It is evident that Bastiat has not clearly discriminated between *value* and *valuation*. "Value," he says, "implies comparison, appreciation, *valuation*, measure." And he thus defines value: "value is the relation (*rapport*) of two services exchanged."

In another place, after recounting a variety of human wants, and remarking that their gratification always gives rise to value because it necessitates an exchange of services, he proceeds to say that had he passed in review the whole catalogue of our wants, he would have found nothing inconsistent with the idea that value is created by exchange alone; to use his own language, he " would have found materials frequently, sometimes forces furnished *gratuitously*, by nature; but human services always exchanging themselves for other human services, reciprocally measuring, rating, appraising, *valuing* themselves one by another, and exhibiting the sole result of that valuation, or VALUE.*

---

* Bastiat's Complete Works, Vol. VI. p. 166. The original, with context, will be found in Appendix B.

Is it not clear that the *object* of "*évaluation*," comparison, or appraisal, must be something else than the "*result*" of that process? That something is [illegible] the amount or quantity of which is ascer-[illegible] by "measuring" it with other values, but the pr[illegible]s of measuring and creating differ widely fr[illegible]ch other. Professor Perry, in his "Political Ec[illegible]my," holds and illustrates, at some length, the sa[illegible] ideas of value. "Strictly speaking, value is n[illegible] quality of any one thing, but a relation which o[illegible]ing holds to another thing. * * * * * T[illegible]e crew of a boat, abandoned at sea, among w[illegible]n the last biscuit has been rationed out, a b[illegible]g of gold belonging to one of the men would not [illegible] purchase a biscuit belonging to another. The [illegible]herent qualities of gold are present. It is sti[illegible] a[illegible] yel[illegible] and heavy; but valuable it is not. [illegible] not purchase anything. Value is not an i[illegible]here[illegible] a[illegible]nd i[illegible]variable attribute; but is the relative powe[illegible] [illegible]ich one thing has of purchasing other things." [illegible]alue, then, has reference to effects, to services; is measurable in, and exchangeable for, these." *

Now, nobody pretends that value is imperishable or indestructible; hence it cannot be an "*invariable* attribute;" nor is it necessary to its existence as a

* Perry's "Political Economy," pp. 34, 38.

quality or property imparted to material things by labor or effort, that it should be invariable. If "values, strictly speaking," are simply "relations," then *relations* should be exchangeable for *things* possessing value, because these things will satisfy human wants and are unobtainable without effort or labor. But what sort of an equation can be constructed from these elements?

We cannot say such or such *quantity of relations* = $100, nor that any amount of relations = 100 pounds of flour; but we can say 1 oz. of gold = 15 oz. of silver = 300 pounds of iron = 2000 pounds of hay = 4000 pounds or 2 tons of coal = 2 cords of wood. But to what property or quality common to all these commodities does the sign of equality relate? Obviously, not to bulk nor to weight as such, for on either of these bases of comparison the relation of gold to wood or coal would be as one to tens of thousands, instead of one to one; nor to hardness nor color, nor to any other property or quality common to all material things—for the variation tested by any such bases of comparison would be almost infinite or would altogether defy precise mathematical statement.

It follows, of necessity, that the property or quality of which equality is affirmed, is a something which bears no fixed or definite relation to matter generally, nor to any one of its physical properties; but it also follows that it is a something of which *quantity* or *amount* can be predicated and which can be estimated and *measured;* and the amount or quantity of which can be stated in precise mathematical terms. On the opposite and now current theory, that "value is a ratio — an external relation"* to quote the language of the author who would banish the phrase "intrinsic value" from economical nomenclature as a mischievous fiction, what meaning attaches to his own statement, that the "Bank of England, warned by experience, weighs rigidly every single sovereign paid in by its customers and does not credit them with more than its *intrinsic value* as bullion?" Undoubtedly there is a "relation" between one sovereign of standard weight and another sovereign of short weight. Yet that value does not attach to weight of itself, it is quite unnecessary to affirm; since, were the fact otherwise an addition of alloy would bring up the sovereign of short weight to the value of the standard coin. But on the theory here propounded—that value is a quality or property resulting from the joint action of labor and the natural forces, aided by capital and directed to the production of commodities required to supply the wants of man—the statement

* McLeod's "Theory of Banking," Vol. I. p. 50.

becomes intelligible and the terms employed are recognized as appropriate. Tried by this test, a small weight of gold is equal to a larger weight of silver, to a still more considerable but varying weight of hay, coal, wood, and other commodities.

An object of known or given weight bears a relation to all other ponderous bodies; so a given measure or quantity of fluid bears a relation to all other fluids; and a given distance bears a relation to all other distances. In either case the known quantity may become the measure of the unknown; and thus its "relation," before indefinite or unknown, becomes definite or known. The same general proposition is true of value; given a thing of known value—as a dollar or any article or commodity possessing admitted, definite value, and it becomes the measure of all other values to which this given, known, or admitted value, may be applied or compared. The commodity of given value, being made by the fact of comparison, a standard by which other values are measured, its "relation" to all other values so compared becomes known, specific, and susceptible of mathematical expression.

But it should be remarked that "relations" subsist only between things which possess, or are assumed to possess, like properties. Thus, between a gallon and a mile—or between a dollar and a ton's weight, it would be absurd to assert there exists a "relation." But between a mile and the mean diameter of the earth's orbit, as also between one dollar and a hundred dollars, or between one dollar and the aggregate wealth of a nation, there either exists a known "relation," or, the "relation" in either case can be accurately or approximately ascertained — certainly there can be no difficulty in *stating* it in terms which would convey to the mind a definite and intelligible idea.

Thus, it will be observed, that in the cases cited —as in all cases it is possible to cite—things to be related must precede "relations" between them; and, in so far as being or existence is concerned, they must be quite independent of such "relations." And it also appears that as a line or stick of known length is required to measure distance or length— that is, to determine the "relations" of the hitherto unknown distance or length to the known; and as a vessel of known capacity is required to measure a certain class of quantities—that is to determine their "relations," so a known or given value is required to measure other values—that is to determine or ascertain the "relations" which exist between the known or given value and any or all other values.

It has been objected to this notion of value—that is, of value except as a "relation"—and especially of the idea of a standard or measure of value, that there is no material which does not, from time to time, change in value; and that a standard or measure should be unchangeable. The fact that all values change, and consequently that an unchangeable standard or measure is impossible of realization, is incontestable. But it is also a fact that all measures of length and capacity are liable to change with varying temperature. Unquestionably the changes in this latter class of measures are less in degree than the changes in the former class. Yet the fact remains that the difference between the two classes is one of degree and not of kind; that is, both are liable to change, and if change renders one class unfit to perform its usual functions, so it must unfit the other to perform its functions.*

Briefly on the boat and its contents: the bag of gold will not, under the special calamitous circumstances assumed, exchange for a biscuit. Therefore, not only is the bag of gold destitute of

---

* The French system of weights and measures does, indeed, theoretically, afford an unchangeable standard; but the moment the theory is reduced to practice the objections above noted attach to all the material things used for the purpose of weighing and measuring.

value, but coined gold generally, and under all circumstances, is necessarily destitute of value. Apply the same process of reasoning to the unfortunate crew about to perish. They are forever cut off from the field of human activity and industry. Their powers of mind and body can never again be put in requisition to render services to their fellow-men. Therefore, not only are their mental and corporeal faculties valueless, but the faculties of all men under all circumstances are valueless also. "A horse, a horse—my kingdom for a horse!" cried a Prince in extremity. But he offered his kingdom in vain. There was no man present with a horse ready for delivery. Therefore, whatever "value" may be postulated of a kingdom, it must be less than the value of a horse!

Prof. Perry avers that value would never exist if every person satisfied his own wants directly by his own efforts; indeed, this position is a corollary of the definition of value, as given by Bastiat. But a hypothetical case, including no element except such as social history has actually supplied, will, in my opinion, demonstrate clearly that value itself, and very definite ideas of relative value, may exist without an "exchange of services," or any kind of "exchange," as that term is understood in business affairs. A man of large family, amply providing himself for the purpose, settles on a rich prairie, far distant from civilized man. He experiments with the cereals on the untried soil—planting corn, rye, wheat, and oats. By carefully noting the labor and the acreage employed in the production of given quantities of each, and also the effect of each in fattening stock to supply his family with meat, he is enabled to determine, with tolerable accuracy, what these several grains are relatively worth to him for consumption—sale and barter being excluded by the hypothesis. Taking 100 as the basis of comparison, he puts down wheat at 60, rye at 45, corn at 22, and oats at 18. These figures represent no money, but simply his conception of the proportionate worth to him for his own use, of given quantities of his several products. He therefore regulates his production of the cereals as nearly as practicable by this scale; and his production of these and all other things is limited to the satisfaction of the wants of himself and those dependent upon him. Years roll on, and civilization, with its railroads, its stores of luxuries to supply wants unknown to pioneer life, and its markets for all the products of human industry, finally reaches the home of the long isolated patriarch. And now a new state of things arises. Hitherto he has formed and been governed by *his own* estimate of the relative importance, worth, utility, beneficial uses, etc., to himself and family, of wheat, corn, etc., due regard being had to the labor and care necessary for the production of each respectively. What idea do the words relative importance, etc., imply, if not the idea of *value?* They are the expression of a *fact* — that, in the opinion of the sole arbiter, the articles named differ in their respective capacities to satisfy the wants of man; that a given quantity of one is, when tried by this standard, equivalent to a larger quantity of the other. There is no word in our language that describes this *fact* so well as value; the articles compared by this man, he being the only judge, differ in *value* in the proportions represented by the scale above given. Hitherto his opinion of the relative values of his products, standing alone, was necessarily his rule of action in his moderately diversified industry. But now the railroad has furnished him with a *market* for any surplus products he may possess, and also with the *market reports.* These reports embody the average collective opinion of the world as to the *relative values* of wheat, corn, rye, and oats. His opinion as to their relative values for his own uses, based on careful observation, was correct; but other lands more favored by nature than his own, produce some of the cereals more abundantly with the same outlay;

and he finds it advantageous to procure these by exchanging such of his products as he had placed lower in his, than they are placed in the world's comparative scale, for others which he had placed higher; and he exchanges them accordingly. But does *value* now, for the first time, attach to his products? They possessed the same power of satisfying the wants of man before, that they possess now. Their relative value—based on the efforts they respectively had cost him and their adaptation to his uses—had been represented by a scale which a *wider comparison* compels him to *revise;* and that is all the effect on the values he had produced, which his exchanging them for values produced by others can possibly exert. The values must be created—they must have an existence—before an exchange of values is possible. A sale or exchange of property implies the concurrence of two parties in estimating its value; but such exchange creates no new thing or quality. At most it establishes a " relation ! "

In another place the author explains value thus:

" Value is not an attribute of any one thing, but a relation subsisting between two things." *

This is another illustration of the impossibility

* Perry's " Political Economy," p. 82.

of so defining value as to make it a nonentity, without at least implying that it is the very opposite—a real actual substantial "thing." For what are the "two things" between which a "relation subsists," if they are "not attributes," or qualities, or properties in some way allied to other "two things," which are themselves certainly not simply relations. Translated into what must be equivalent language, if value is correctly defined in the extract quoted, the definition would read thus: "Value is not an attribute of any one thing, but a relation subsisting between two relations."

On the next preceding page the author has evidently experienced even greater difficulty in annihilating value as a distinct entity, by means of a definition. "Value," says he, "is a relative word. It is usually defined as purchasing power, that is to say, the value of anything is its power of purchasing other things." Very well; "power" is a measurable *something*, instead of being what he affirms value is—a virtual nothing, of which even "the notion is not conceivable, except by a comparison," etc.

He proceeds, "it is not an independent quality of one thing, as hardness is a quality of a stone, but it is *a quality of one thing*, as estimated in *a corresponding quality* of something else."

This definition, though defective, is so far correct that it asserts the existence of value as a "quality" of things, instead of being simply "a relation subsisting between things." Had he said "value is a quality of one thing which is estimated in a corresponding quality of something else," his definition would have been less defective. The word "estimated" conveys the idea of comparing different values for the purpose of measuring them, and of thus ascertaining, and defining with accuracy and precision, "the relations subsisting between them."

The writer here quoted appears to deem it an important fact that "value is not an independent quality;" as if it would hence follow that it is not a "quality" at all, but admits that it is a *dependent* "quality." The fact still remains that it is a quality of things, and not simply "a relation" between "a quality of one thing and a corresponding quality of something else." It seems to me utterly impossible for the human intellect to confound the idea of "relation" here, with the idea of a quality and a corresponding quality pertaining to two different objects, between which the fact of relation is affirmed; or, in other words, it seems impossible for the human intellect to regard these two corresponding qualities on the one hand, and the relations subsisting between them on the other, as the same identical fact or thing.

A recent writer holds, that whereas, of the three elements that enter into the production of new commodities possessing value, viz.: capital, labor, and the natural forces, the latter is a passive element which the possessor of capital utilizes in industrial operations in such manner as he may judge best for his own interest; and, as this element can, of itself add nothing to the wealth of a country, therefore it may properly be excluded from business considerations and economical discussions. This partial view of the subject is not wanting in plausibility; and it is practically correct, if limited in its application to the case of a capitalist seeking to invest his means in some profitable undertaking. But a partial view of a subject will hardly warrant a general conclusion. A somewhat analogous argument has been used to prove that interest on money is wrong:—put two pieces of coin in a sack and let them lie there a century, and they will not produce another! Therefore it is labor that *produces* all wealth, and all interest on money is extortion and a violation of the rights of labor! But with equal pertinency and force it may be retorted that labor, subjected to the same conditions—that is, if entirely cut off from any aid from either capital or natural forces—could never produce the smallest value; on the contrary, its continued existence would be impossible. Of course the conditions here assumed can never be realized in a world composed of matter, every particle of which is instinct with force, of which no human power can divest it; but if these conditions are unrealizable, they are not unthinkable. Apply the same conditions to labor and capital combined, or to capital and the natural forces combined—excluding the natural forces in the former hypothesis and labor in the latter—and the same negative result would necessarily follow: there would be no creation of new values—no production. In either hypothesis there is one of the two indispensable elements or factors of production wanting—the natural forces in the former and labor in the latter. Restore the missing element in either case, and you have, in a generalized form, all the enginery of production in every department of human industry.

The second proposition is, that the natural forces available to man in the work of production differ in amount, efficiency or intensity in different countries and in various portions of the same country. Perhaps it may be allowable to assume a hypothetical common *unit of force*, applicable to both elements—labor and natural forces; as then, the proposition slightly changed, could be stated thus:—the *propor-*

tion of labor and the natural forces varies in different countries and in sections of the same country. Thus, the amount of natural force stored in the coal beds of England and the State of Pennsylvania, is greater than that of a like force stored in any other portions of the world, of the same dimensions.

This remark applies more especially to the first form of the proposition. To illustrate the second form—yet it has a distinct bearing on the first—let us take the gold mines of California and Australia at an early day, and compare them with the gold mines of Georgia, the Carolinas and the Ural Mountains. The proportion of gold to the number of miners (as also the *amount*) in the former cases was much greater than in the latter. So, too, the natural forces which contribute to the production of the cereals, are greater in the aggregate in the United States than in Great Britain; as well as much greater in *proportion* to the amount or sum of the labor element. This general proposition will, on a very little reflection, be recognized as applicable to all forms of industry in every country.

For instance, the same labor will produce more cotton (in value) in our Gulf States than in Egypt or India; more of Indian corn in the Western States than in any part of Europe; more of silk in France than in America; more of certain kinds of manufactures in England than in any other part of the world. The labor, skill, capital, and all other accessories may be the same in the several cases assumed; but the result, taking either quantity or value as the standard, will be different.

The necessary conclusion would seem to be that the principal cause of the difference must consist in the varying proportion, sum or efficiency of the natural forces, which, in the cases assumed, assisted, and whose assistance was indispensable, in the work of production.

The principle asserted in this proposition has, in all ages and countries, controlled the action of the great mass of mankind in their efforts to procure subsistence or to acquire wealth. It has prompted all migrations, both of individuals and of tribes, excepting only the predatory and the religious; and the ignorant not less than the intelligent have universally, though unconsciously, obeyed its dictates. The unlettered laborer of Western Europe has heard that he can do better for himself and his family by migrating to the new world; indeed he knows that many no better off than himself in their former home have become wealthy in the land whither he is going. The question for political economy to answer is—how or why can he improve his condition by removing from one country to another? His capital and the labor at his disposal are definite and fixed quantities. It will take a goodly portion of the former to pay the expenses of himself and family to their new home. His labor force on reaching it will be the same as when he started; but his capital will be materially diminished. What can compensate for his loss of time and money? Simply the fact that he secures here a much larger or more efficient co-operation of the natural forces in the work of production; with less capital and the same labor as barely enabled him to live in densely-peopled Europe, he now produces a surplus and paves his way to wealth. Our own people spend millions a year in transporting themselves and families from the North and East to the South and West—from comparatively crowded to thinly-peopled or unoccupied regions. They fully understand the *practical effect* of the principle under consideration, and nothing more. They expect to secure a larger or more effective co-operation of the natural forces in the raising of wheat or corn or cotton, or in mining, than they could realize where population is more abundant, and the natural forces are, to a great extent, appropriated; and they anticipate advantages from this source that will far more than compensate them for all incidental expenses and privations. The farmer is governed by the same principle when he plants one piece of land with corn, another with potatoes, another with wheat, and so on through the list of his products. In every instance his aim is to plant a certain piece of land with such grain or other crop as will enable him to profit most by nature's co-operation.

The manufacturer brings to the study of this question in the concrete, a more varied knowledge and a higher order of intelligence. He depends upon nature for motive power, for the bleaching of some products and the imparting of delicate colors to others; and he selects a locality with reference to a water-fall, or the proximity of coal, as also to the dryness or humidity of climate, the purity of water, etc., etc., in order that he may have the co-operation of the natural forces to the fullest extent in perfecting his products. The same general remarks are applicable to all men engaged in productive industry of whatever kind; for the same general principle applies to all industrial operations in all countries.

It is a fact familiar to all, that several lots of gold of given weight and fineness, though mined respectively in each of the four quarters of the globe, possess the same value in any one of the great marts of the commercial world. An ounce of one lot may have cost the Russian miner ten days' labor; an ounce of another lot may have cost the California miner but the labor of a single day; another ounce may have cost a less fortunate Californian five days' labor—and so on through a scale of wide variation. But the cost to the individual producer does not control the value of gold. The ounce that is the product of full ten days of hard labor, is worth no more than the ounce that was mined in a single day. The value of each approximates the estimated *average cost* of producing one ounce of gold. Substitute given weights of wheat, the products of various countries, or of cotton wool or iron: substitute given quantities of each of the innumerable fabrics and other commodities which man's industry and enterprise are constantly placing on the markets of the world,—substitute each of these in turn, for the ounce of standard gold (assuming a standard of quality as in the case of gold), and the same reasoning will apply and will conduct to the same result.

The value of any single product would bear only an *incidental* relation to its cost. The value of *all* the products of a given kind and quality, would approximate the cost of *all in the aggregate;* and hence the value of *each* product would necessarily approximate the *mean or average* cost of all the class of products to which it belongs; and on this basis all are bought and sold or exchanged.

The principles here laid down, clearly include and in my opinion effectually dispose of, the hypothetical diamond problem of Bastiat, which has been adopted and wrought up by Prof. Perry in his Political Economy.* A man strolling on the sea shore by a "happy chance," finds a large diamond of pure water. Here, then, is a thing possessing great value which costs little or no labor; therefore labor is not necessarily an element of value. Such in brief is the substance of the case cited to prove that values may be produced without the agency of labor. But it may be remarked in the first instance that the case is simply hypothetical; and that it would be time enough to consider its bearing on a scientific question when the correctness of the hypothesis should be attested by its conversion into reality. Waiving this point, however, and admitting that the finding of a diamond and realizing thereby great value at no cost of labor or other values is a fact; it will scarcely be asserted that one fact, exceptional in character and standing alone, is an adequate basis for the enunciation of a new principle. The exceptional feature of the fact consists in the diamond's being acquired by chance instead of labor devoted to mining. But the diamond itself is precisely like all other diamonds of best quality. Hence it can be

* See his "Political Economy," p. 43.

classified and made to play its part as the basis of a broad generalization. Many diamonds must have cost the miner more than their value at the place of production; others have cost less; and here is one which cost nothing. The cost of all in the aggregate fixes the value of each, and they come under the same law as cotton, grain, and gold, the products of mines and soils of varying richness and fertility.

The given product of known quality is now invested with a standard value—the average cost (in which are always supposed to be included ordinary profits) of producing all like products, reference being had to a given time and place. Success in the work of production, then, must depend upon this one condition—the ability of the producer to place his produce upon the market at a cost not exceeding the average cost of all similar products. Labor and the natural forces being the two necessary elements or factors of production and the former being fixed and limited in quality, while as regards the latter there is no known or assignable limit to the modes nor to the extent and efficiency of their co-operation with man, he necessarily, as he also does instinctively, seeks to make such co-operation more and more effective by availing himself of the best arrangements which his intelligence and his means enable him to make, in order to render the labor and capital at his disposal most fruitful in the production of values.

A recent British authority already referred to, scouts the idea that value has any other than an accidental relation to labor. "Labor is in no way whatever the cause of, or even necessary to, value; and in fact in this commercial country the enormously greater portion of valuable things are not the produce of labor at all." * * "Here it is quite clear that we have now got the true source and cause of value. It is DEMAND. Value is not a quality of an object but an affection of the mind. The sole source and origin of value is human desire. When there is a demand for things, they have value; when the demand ceases, they cease to have value." * One element of value is here wanting. The "things" which are objects of "human desire" must be unobtainable without effort or labor in order to "have value." Air, water, sun-light and heat are objects of "human desire;" yet as they, under ordinary conditions, cost no labor, they do not "have value." The "valuable things not the produce of labor at all" to which he refers, are chiefly various forms of *credit*, which would require too much space to discuss at length. There is a difference between a dollar in coin and a note which entitles the holder

---

* McLeod's "Theory of Banking," Vol. I. pp. 56, 57.

to demand a dollar from the maker of the note, which science cannot fail to recognize.* But if value is simply "an affection of the mind," what are riches? In what do they consist and how should they be defined? They are generally considered as meaning the ownership of a large amount of valuable property—or a large accumulation of values in some form or other. The definition of value above given would scarcely admit of such accumulations.

Again: a man becoming weary with labor requires water, bread and meat to refresh himself and restore his flagging energies. Hence there arises on his part a "demand" for each of these articles. He knows that water is so abundant all around him

* For instance, the writer quoted vol. i. p. 50, says: "Value is a ratio—an external relation. What can be the *representative* of a ratio, or of an external relation." On the same page the author speaking of bank notes and their value, says: "it is not exactly these bits of paper that have value. What is really of value is the Right or Property to demand money." Is the word "value" there the synonym of "ratio" or "external relation?" If we should say "what is really of *ratio ;*" or "what is really of *external relation* is the right to demand money," nobody would understand us. "The right to demand money" is recognized here as a thing "of value." It necessarily follows that money itself must be "of value" at least equal to "the right to demand money ;" or to use the words of the author it must necessarily "have value." The abstract idea which such language gives rise to is not a relation or ratio, but a thing, a peculiar property or quality of the particular object spoken of. Ask *how much* "value" it "has" and the idea of "ratio or relation" is at once evoked; and you now have the idea of "relation" to other values, of valuation, or of the measuring of values by some standard—which is generally but not necessarily money.

that he can get all he requires without buying it.
But his reason teaches him that bread and meat for
his repast are not produced by nature alone; that
they cost labor, skill, self-denial to *somebody;* yet he
desires them and must have them or he must perish;
the "demand" can be abated in no other way than
by the satisfaction of his wants—of his cravings for
food. After more or less of parleying with a victual-
ler, his "mind" finally assents to the proposition,
that the "demand" of two shillings, or the equivalent of an hour's labor, for bread and meat to satisfy
his wants, is a fair one; so he pays that sum for a
frugal meal, and the transaction is finished by an
exchange of commodities recognized by both parties
to be of equal value. Now did "the mind" *produce*
the values which enter into this transaction; or did
"the mind" of the laborer simply *perceive* or recognize the fact, that there are properties in bread and
meat of which he must necessarily avail himself to
maintain health and life; that these properties are
unobtainable without effort or labor; and that his
money was but a fair equivalent for the quantity of
bread and meat which he required for his meal?
In other words, did "the mind" "create" the values
"out of nothing," or create them in any way or
sense; or did it simply perceive and recognize values
already produced; and having recognized their ex-

istence, did not "the mind" merely compare and measure them, one with the other? "The mind" by the aid of the different senses perceives color, hardness, weight and heat, in different material objects. By means of various contrivances, it measures the degree or intensity of those properties attaching to any particular object submitted to its inspection. Does it hence follow that heat, or color, or weight, "resides exclusively in the mind?"

The same writer cites the sale of land in London at £2,000,000 an acre as an instance of the existence of immense values which "are not in any way whatever the result of labor at all." The bare fact does not seem to me to warrant the conclusion. The sites of modern cities are generally selected with reference to a commodious harbor, or a large water power, or the confluence of navigable rivers ramifying a fertile country, the intersection of great railway lines, etc., etc. Whatever cause may have induced the selection of the site, the very fact of its selection implies that the same cause is expected to attract thither large numbers of people. Suppose a sagacious man foreseeing the profitable uses to which the great natural advantages of the place can be devoted, buys the land at $100 per acre, and proceeds to erect mills, warehouses, etc., to meet the anticipated wants of the neighboring country. People begin to avail themselves of the facilities he has provided for their accommodation; and the foundation of the future city is securely laid. Presently a country shop-keeper, observing that people are flocking to the new town, proposes to remove his stock of goods thither. He accordingly applies to the owner of the land for a lot on which to build a house and store, and he finds himself obliged to pay $100 for an eighth of an acre or abandon his purpose. Which alternative to adopt is the question for him to decide. So he reasons over the matter thus: "This lot of land is in precisely the same condition as when the present owner bought it; yet he demands an advance of seven hundred per cent. on the price he paid for it. Why should he ask it, and why should I pay such an enormous profit—simply that he should benefit by it? But—after all I can sell many more goods here where there are so many people from all quarters every day in the year, and make much more money than I can in my country shop. Moreover, the lot will probably advance on my hands as population increases and local industries multiply; so I will take it at the price he has put upon it." The principle involved in this transaction underlies all similar transactions; and they are necessarily incident to the growth of cities.

The buyer of the lot, in this case, takes $100

which he has gained in his country store and pays the seller $87.50 profit on an investment of $12.50; in other words, he transfers that sum to the seller for what cost him nothing. There has been a distribution of values previously existing; there has been, however, no creation of new values. But it will be said the buyer got property worth what it cost him—the trade was simply an exchange of equal values. The truth of this proposition must be admitted but with an important qualification. The value named here, consists in the privilege of sharing in the *natural advantages* of the location, which, under our social system, a man may appropriate and then compel others to pay for or forego their use. This fact seems to me clearly an evil for which no adequate cure has yet been found. It operates as a disturbing force in the distribution of wealth or values already acquired or produced, as damaging to the mass of producers as a whole, as it is advantageous to the smaller class who profit by it.

But it seems equally clear that selling and re-selling the same things every time at advanced prices, which have been subjected to no change of character, place or condition, cannot possibly give rise to new values or add one farthing to the aggregate wealth of the world. If new values can be thus created, then private fortunes and national wealth may be indefinitely increased by a harmless and easy process, involving no labor; for the production of wealth injures nobody directly or indirectly.

In the case under consideration, the shop-keeper transferring his business from the country to the town raises his price-list with reference to his larger investment or higher rent, taking proper account of the addition to his trade accruing from his new location; and he thus makes his customers indemnify him for the profit he was obliged to pay the owner of the soil, on his little lot. The fact, however, remains that the original owner of the land, when its fitness and natural advantages for a town site were first recognized, is enabled to sell it out in parcels at rates of profit corresponding to the more or less sanguine anticipations of the purchasers, and without expending any money or labor to add to its value.

On the hypothesis under consideration, the mills or warehouses built by the land-owner for the purpose of attracting business and starting the projected town, themselves participate in the general "rise of property;" he is therefore more than compensated for his outlay by the appreciation of these structures, while their existence and activity inspire confidence in the future and make his town lots more eagerly sought for at higher and still higher prices. The period arrives in the growth of all towns when taxes are levied to make public improvements; such charges affect the selling price of, and the profits realized upon, town lots; but they have no necessary relation to the abstract question under consideration.

The same principles that are involved in the case of the nascent city, apply also to countries possessing large tracts of fertile land in its natural state. Under a mistaken or iniquitous land system, the shrewd capitalist is enabled to buy, at "government price," immense tracts just beyond the bounds of cultivation, or take up vast wooded districts, or other tracts so situated with reference to navigable waters or projected railways, that they must soon become the centre of local commerce and large populations, and then wait for the labor of the advancing multitude to render them "valuable." As a rule, these speculators simply hold their lands and do nothing to improve them. There they lie in the same state as they were in the time of Columbus; but the hardy settler must pay the sagacious holder five or ten times the government price; *or* pass over the broad belt of speculators' territory, and by cultivating land beyond it, impart to it still further value. The lands are finally sold and paid for with money earned, perhaps, in Europe or in the Atlantic States. The values of which that money is the embodiment, pass from those who produced them to others who produced nothing—save, possibly, the original purchase money. And since the landholders in this case produce nothing, the sum of previously existing values is not increased by the profits they realized on their lands. That sum remains the same—having simply been subjected (in part) to a re-distribution.

"When a country employs credit, it is just so much the richer by an equal amount of the precious metals." *

"Bullion is the only true promise to pay." "It is quite evident that the promises to pay floating in a nation, must bear some proportion in quantity to the actual quantity of bullion. It is quite impossible to fix any definite proportion. * * Experience is the only guide on the subject." †

"To say that money, because it is material and the produce of labor, has *intrinsic* value, and that a bank note is only the representative of value, is just as absurd as to say that a wooden yard-measure is *intrinsic* distance and that the space of 36 inches between two points is *representative* distance." ‡

* McLeod's "Theory of Banking," Vol. I. p. 76.
† Ib., Vol. II. p. 192.   ‡ Ib., Vol. I. p. 50.

A banker loans a manufacturer $10,000—$9000 in bank notes, and $1000 in coin. Soon after this transaction, he converts all his assets into coin, and absconds, taking it with him to parts unknown. The $9000 in bank notes at once become worthless; while the $1000 in coin still retain their original "value." Indeed, they are worth a trifle more, because the dollar of account has slightly appreciated by the extinction of $9000 in paper money. At this stage no government, however powerful, could divest the coin of value, nor impart value to the paper money of the broken bank. The truth of these propositions has been frequently demonstrated in the financial history of States. The State may pay the losses of the note holders, by taxing the rest of its citizens for that purpose; but it cannot invest the worthless notes with value.

Now, it is perfectly clear that the value of the coin, and the "value" of the notes at the time the loan was effected, were essentially different in kind, quality, or character. For that difference, in whatever it consists, or to whatever attributable, there should be a name; or, at least, there should be a way of describing or defining the two kinds of value. The "value" of the notes, it is admitted, consists in "the right to demand money." Hence, it may be termed commercial, representative, or conditional value—the condition referring to the contingent payment or non-payment of the notes when presented for redemption. The coin dollars " have value " of which no contingency, fraud, or failure, can divest them. Hence, it is actual, unconditional, permanent, real value; and being inseparable from the coin, it must be pervasive or intrinsic.

A few more points made by this author are worthy of consideration in this connection. Having cited vast improvements and manufacturing enterprises successfully carried on by means of the Scotch system of cash credits, he says, " hence we see that the mere will of man has *created* vast masses of wealth out of *nothing*, and then DECREATED them into NOTHING." " They (i. e., the cash credits) are created for the express purpose of *creating or forming future* products, which would either have had no existence at all but for them, or, at all events, it would have been deferred for a very long period, until solid money could have been obtained to produce them."*

The " future products," when " created and formed " through the agency of labor, for which the cash credit provides a way to obtain subsistence, implements, etc., may constitute " vast masses of wealth." But the credit itself, however large it may

* McLeod's " Theory of Banking," Vol. I. p. 138.

be, would find no place in a correct inventory of personal or national wealth, for the reason that it is not wealth. It will enable the banker to add to his wealth to the extent of the interest he receives on these " incorporeal entities created out of nothing;" and the contractor also may (and he may not) add to his wealth. But these " future " gains must be contingent upon the success of the projected enterprise.

"There is an enormous mass of valuable property created by the mere will of the Legislature, such as copyrights."* A book, or an engraving, is the product of human labor, mental and physical — Nature's materials and forces always co-operating; if it meets a public want, it is " valuable property," because it can be published and sold at a profit.

The law of copyright simply provides in substance, that if a man produces values of this kind, they shall be the property of the producer—the same as is the case with corn, and all other valuable products. The Legislature can makes laws to protect property from spoliators and thieves; but it cannot create wealth out of nothing. The existence of property is older than human statutes; and the idea of ownership, and of the rights it confers, is shared in common by infant and adult, by savage and

* McLeod's "Theory of Banking," Vol. I. p. 189.

civilized man. Moreover, it is certain not only that property in authorship, but violations of the rights of such property, must have been known and recognized long before any law of copyright was enacted to protect it.

A few words on this author's remarks on labor will close the discussion of this branch of the subject. Taking for his text "the popular doctrine that labor is the cause of value," he proceeds to argue that it is absurd, by a series of what he regards as equivalent propositions. If this doctrine is true, "the value [of a product] must be proportional to the labor;" "a thing once produced by labor, must always have value, and the same value;" "all variations in value must be due to variations in labor;" "all things produced by the same amount of labor, must be of equal value;" "and lastly, whatever [object] labor has been bestowed upon, must have value." *

It will not be forgotten that the proposition it is my aim to establish, is, that labor is one of two elements, the joint action of which is necessary to the production of wealth or value. But it may be worth while to show that the reasoning (the points only of which are given above) against the doctrine that labor is the sole cause of value, is by no means

* McLeod's "Theory of Banking," Vol. I. pp. 53, 55.

conclusive—especially since it has an indirect bearing upon my own.

The author quoted holds that "debts are wealth," * and he places credits, annuities, insurance policies, the public funds, etc., in the same category —citing them as proofs of his doctrine, that vast masses of wealth are produced by the "human will," or by "legislative fiat," without the agency of labor.

If his method is sound and correct, it would follow from his premises that all debts add to the general wealth in proportion to their respective amounts, and the same may be said of credits, funds, etc. But he would be justified in replying to such an "argument," that his propositions are qualified by conditions, which, if not in all cases stated, are necessarily implied; that the proceeds of credit may be wasted, or injudiciously invested; and that debts may ruin the creditor without special advantages to anybody; and hence, they would not add to the wealth of the country. So, too, whether labor be the sole cause of value, or one of two elements, or factors, which are indispensable to the production of value, it by no means follows that given activity of one, or both, would necessarily produce values— much less equal values—under all circumstances.

* McLeod's "Theory of Banking," Vol. I. p. 179.

Labor spent in planting corn in Sahara, or in mining for gold in Pennsylvania, or England, would produce no value. But labor devoted to mining gold in California, or iron and coal in Pennsylvania or England, or in raising corn in our Western States, provided it be directed by intelligence and furnished with the proper accessories, would produce values in abundance. The production of value, then, requires other conditions than the mere co-operation or joint activity of labor and the forces and materials which Nature supplies; but, given all other conditions it is possible to conceive, yet there can be, in my opinion, no creation of new values if such co-operation or joint activity is wanting.

The casual reader may very naturally think that too much consideration has already been given to a few of the specific modes by which it is alleged wealth and new values can be and are actually created without the agency of human labor; but the issue which this allegation presents, is a most important, if not indeed, a vital one. For if it is demonstrable that the "human will," or the "fiat of the Legislature," or the agreement of two or more parties, constituting debts and credits, or the issue of paper money, or the putting forth of government bonds, or of insurance policies, or any other unnamed device, does or can, altogether independently of labor, actually produce new values, by "creating wealth out of nothing," then it becomes a serious question whether a "protective tariff" does not also belong in the same category, and possess the same faculty or power of "creating wealth out of nothing," and bestowing upon man objects or things of value which minister to his happiness, but which man's labor had no agency in producing. A still further question arises: if wealth can be "created out of nothing," without the agency of labor, is there any positive limit to the *amount* which may be thus created? And yet another:—if, by certain modes or processes already known, wealth can be thus created, is it not reasonable to assume that an indefinite number of new processes to effect like results remain to be discovered? Sufficient wealth places at the disposal of its possessor everything that the world affords to satisfy his wants; may not these wealth-creating processes ultimately become so numerous and productive as to enable man to forego toil altogether, without in the least diminishing the number and variety of objects which contribute to his happiness, or curtailing his means of acquiring them?

—Recurring to the "wealth created out of nothing," which it is alleged resides in bank notes and other forms of credit, and to the admission that such value consists in "the right to demand money," a moment's reflection will convince the intelligent and attentive economist, that the so-called creation of wealth out of nothing, is simply an actual or contingent transfer of wealth; and that the several modes of "creation" above specified, all belong in one category. "The right to demand" a dollar of a banker, does not create a dollar; cash credits, "created for the express purpose of creating or forming future products," are not themselves "products" in the sense in which that term is used; a government bond, or an insurance policy, vests in the holder "the right to demand" a given amount of money at a specified time, or on the happening of a contingency therein described; but the money, when paid, is simply *transferred* from one party to another party; and the sum of money or of values previously existing, is neither increased nor diminished by the operation.

Credits—especially bank notes, when they are accepted as a "circulating medium" and perform more or less perfectly the functions of money—constitute a FACT of which political economy must take cognizance. They may sometimes stimulate industry, and increase the production of values—perhaps at the expense of an equitable distribution of the results of industry. On the other hand, credits too often promote speculation, encourage idleness, and diminish production; but in no case do credits of themselves, under any form, add to the aggregate real or "intrinsic" values of any country, or of the world at large.

PROPERTY IN LAND.

"Not only have present land tenures an indefensible origin, but it is impossible to discover any mode in which land *can* become private property." *

"The world is God's bequest to mankind. All men are joint heirs to it." †

"It cannot be apportioned as private property among all adult males who have reached twenty-one on a special day; for, if so, what is to become of those who come of age on the morrow? Is it proposed that each man, woman, and child shall have a section? If so, what becomes of all who are to be born next year? * *   Until we can demonstrate that men born after a certain date are doomed to slavery, we must consider that no such allotment is permissible." ‡

"Ethical truth is as exact and as peremptory as physical truth; in this matter of land tenure the verdict of morality must be distinctly *yea* or *nay*.

* Herbert Spencer's "Social Statics," p. 134.
† Ib., p. 136.   ‡ Ib., p. 138.

Either men *have* a right to make the soil private property, or they *have not*. There is no medium. We must choose one of two positions. There can be no half-and-half opinion." *

Mr. Spencer not only excepts to Locke's theory that appropriating and mixing one's labor with a natural product make such product, thus removed from the state of nature, his property; but he contends that "no one can, by the mere act of appropriating to himself any wild unclaimed animal or fruit, supersede the joint claims of other men to it."† The right of the person who caught the animal or gathered the fruit, to possess it, he admits may be better than the right of any *one* man; but not "greater than the pre-existing rights of all other men put together."

Hence his sweeping general conclusion that "his (any man's) title to possession cannot be admitted as a matter of *right*, but only on the ground of convenience;" ‡

"The point to be debated is, whether he had any right to gather or mix his labor with that which by the hypothesis previously belonged to mankind at large." §

Thus it would seem that the institution of pri-

---

* Herbert Spencer's " Social Statics," p. 139.   † Ib., p. 145.
‡ Ib., p. 146.   § Ib., p. 145.

vate property is a usurpation which, if tolerated at all, must necessarily be in derogation of right, and on the plea of convenience. For by the argument there can, under no possible circumstances, be rightful property in land, even in that which the holder may have reclaimed from the sea, nor in any material thing which man may have removed from a state of nature by mixing his labor with and imparting value to it. And it is clear that there can be no material property which does not attach to the earth or some of its products.

Spencer very justly remarks that Proudhon and his party betray themselves into an "awkward dilemma" by the assertion that "all property is robbery;" for it hence "follows that a man can have no right to the things he consumed for food," and therefore "a man has no property in his own flesh and blood—can have no valid title to himself," &c., &c. Do not Spencer's theories, rigidly applied, as he insists they should be, involve their adherents in the same "awkward dilemma?" True, he argues correctly that the "instinct of accumulation and the desire for personal acquisition" "pre-suppose a *right* of private property; for by right we mean that which harmonizes with the human constitution as divinely ordained."

But, the preceding propositions being sound,

that there can be no private property in land; and that man can acquire no right of property in material things by appropriating and mixing his own labor with them; moreover that he has no right to take and use wild unclaimed fruits or game because of the constant presence in all places and at all times of the superior " pre-existing rights of all other men put together:" it would seem to be impossible to acquire, or even to conceive the existence of " private property" to satisfy the unextinguishable "instinct" and " desire for personal acquisition" whose demands to be gratified, he admits, are legitimate. He, however, assumes to show how private property can be acquired without violating any of the principles which he has laid down, and which he holds to be of paramount and perpetual obligation. His plan will be set forth as briefly as possible. " The equal claims of all men to the use of the earth "— "the co-heirship of all men to the soil," constitute its foundation. " Instead of being the possession of individuals, the country would be held by the great corporate body—Society. Instead of leasing his acres from an isolated proprietor, the farmer would lease them from the nation." " Stewards would be public officials instead of private ones, and tenancy the only land tenure." *

* Herbert Spencer's "Social Statics," p. 141.

"Having thus hired a tract of land from his fellow-men for a given period, for understood purposes and on specified terms—having thus obtained for a time the exclusive use of that land by a definite agreement with its owners, it is manifest that an individual may, without the infringement of the rights of others, appropriate to himself that portion of produce which remains after he has paid to mankind the promised rent. He has now, to use Locke's expression, mixed his labor with certain products of the earth, and his claim to them is in this case valid, because he obtained the *consent* of society, before so expending his labor, and having fulfilled the condition which society imposed in giving that consent— the payment of rent—society, to fulfil its part of the agreement, must acknowledge his title to that surplus which remains after the rent has been paid. * * The tenant may equitably claim the supplementary share as his private property; may so claim it without any disobedience to the law of equal freedom; and has therefore a *right* so to claim it." *

Let us see: "Ethical truth is as exact and as peremptory as physical truth." All men are joint owners of the soil; yet, even though all should agree to sell a portion of the soil to one of their number *to-day*, they could not do it without violat-

---

Herbert Spencer's "Social Statics," p. 147.

ing the rights of "those who come of age on the morrow." Then how about society's leasing the soil in parcels for "a given time?" How long may the "given time" of right extend? One year?—ten years?—a hundred years? If "society" has the right to lease land for a "given time," it must have a right to fix the period and the terms of the lease, since there is no other authority over the soil recognized in the theory. Then why may it not lease its trust property for any "given time," from one year to a thousand years? In any event, "what is to be done with those who come of age on the morrow," and who find every acre of soil leased to individuals for a given time,"—longer, perhaps, than they can expect to live? According to the theory of personal rights propounded by Spencer, the rights of "those who come of age on the morrow," and during the entire term of the leases, are ruthlessly violated by the lessors—" the lawful owner, society," or its agents. The *fact* that these young citizens are barred out from their inheritance—an equal share with their fellows in the soil, " God's bequest to mankind "—constitutes their true grievance ; the *form* or *mode* of exclusion, whether by sale or lease of the soil, is to them wholly immaterial, since in either case their rights, according to this theory, are sacrificed, and they are left without remedy.

A theory which would make Robinson Crusoe a trespasser on the rights of "the human race;" which would say to the hardy pioneer of uncultivated regions who subsists on "wild, unclaimed animals and fruits," You "break the law;" which would not allow him to call his own a diamond pebble or a gold nugget which he picks up on a shore hitherto untrodden by man; which holds that the soil "belongs to mankind at large," and is inalienable under any conceivable circumstances; which would invalidate all titles to personal property throughout the whole world, and make private ownership depend upon conditions impossible to realize: this theory is utterly unsound and impracticable; and were it practicable it would necessarily result in anarchy. Strongly as he reprobates communism, it is difficult to see why his theory does not justify it. For if "possession" for a thousand years gives no title; if man cannot make his own any material thing with which he mixes his labor; in short, if, as he asserts, all claims and titles to private property of every nature and kind are a fraud upon "society" and "mankind at large;" and if "equity sternly commands that theory be embodied in fact," then it necessarily follows, first, that of all the holders of property in the whole world, *not one* has a *valid claim* to what he has in possession; and, second, that, all claims and titles to property being illegitimate and invalid, they should be so declared and be disposed of accordingly: the theory should "be embodied in fact." Here, then, we should have—indeed we have *now*, if this theory is correct—a world full of wealth in all its myriad forms, and not a *rightful* individual owner of any portion thereof. "The great corporate body, society," or "mankind at large," is the owner; and, so far as persons are concerned, the right of any one to an interest in any part or all of this wealth is just as good as the right of any and every other. A species of communism would seem to be the necessary consequence of the recognition of this theory; yet far be it from me to impute so pestilent a heresy to this truly great man, or to admit that it is reconcilable with, or not strongly reprobated by, the general tenor of his teachings.

Preliminarily to all this theorizing, Spencer remarks that government originates in man's imperfection, and that it is begotten by necessity out of evil. This view of human government harmonizes with my own. Given, sufficient intelligence on the part of every human being to understand the rights and duties of every human being, associated in all individuals with a spirit of loyalty to the moral law that would render its violation impossible, and no human government would be necessary. Humanity deplores the want of such a degree of intelligence and morality; and governments justify their own existence and the exercise of powers of restraint and coercion, by assuming to supply this defect in the various members of society, and to enforce the law of right as ordained by the Supreme Power. Yet, while such is the theory of human government, in its measures and policies it partakes largely of human imperfection. It has never made a law affecting property which effectually secures to each individual precisely the amount, and no more, which would be his were the moral law universally and rigidly enforced; nor is it supposable that it will ever attain to a perfect standard—since such attainment would imply that government is no longer a necessity.

But meanwhile society is obliged to choose between anarchy and violence, on the one hand, and a system of laws founded on "expediency," yet approaching as nearly as may be to the requirements of natural law, on the other; and thus far society has chosen the latter alternative. These laws recognize the right of man to the ownership of material property in all its various forms, including definite portions of the soil. This right may be described in brief and general terms as resting on original appropriation, labor (imparting value to material objects), and purchase or exchange respectively. The right of sovereignty founded on discovery is simply the application, on a large scale, of the right of appropriating the gifts of nature hitherto unappropriated by man; and whether such right will or will not stand the test of severe criticism, it is a fact which cannot be ignored that all land titles in the new world are based upon it—if not indeed upon the inferior right which conquest from feeble savage tribes is supposed to confer. These titles, even should they be pronounced invalid by the profound speculative philosopher, are not likely ever to be annulled. The same general remarks apply with equal fitness to the ownership of the soil and its products in all countries. Land, with all the natural forces inherent in it, subject to certain rights theoretically reserved by the State, is universally recognized as a form of MATTER which may be appropriated or bought and owned by man as property. It is true he did not and cannot *create* land; but it is equally true that he cannot create matter in any form. Labor directed by intelligence will impart value to various forms of matter—among other forms, to matter which constitutes the soil; that *value* he creates, and it is his by natural law, subject to the equitable rights of his fellow-men, who, by loan of capital or otherwise, have aided him in his work. That value which is his, exists in the concrete; it is inseparable from matter; and man must have a right to private ownership of material property, or, communism, in ownership and management, must of necessity be the only true system of property. This reasoning applies with equal feebleness or force to property in land, and to all other kinds or forms of material property.*

* It is alleged that "an individual can never acquire absolute and sole right in land, but that there is always some limitation of his right and a power of resumption reserved to the State." This proposition is quite needlessly proved by citing the fact that the State takes land for "a road, a canal, or a railroad station," and makes the landowner such "compensation" as in its sovereign discretion it sees fit to award. This well-known fact, however, either does not prove that private property in land is a "usurpation," a "fundamental error," a "crude and monstrous assumption," *or* it proves too much. For, if the fact cited amounts to a demonstration, or even an admission, on the part of the acquiescing people, that there can be no "absolute and sole right [of property] in land," so, by parity of reason, there can be no "*absolute* and sole right" of property in any material substance whatever, nor any right of property in one's own products or earnings, nor even in one's own person. For as "the landowner is unceremoniously forced to give up his land for the public convenience," by the State, so the State alike unceremoniously forces the citizen to "give up" whatever proportion of his property it deems fit to take for public uses. And the State goes so far as to force its citizens to "give up" their personal liberty and their lives on the same plea as it makes in the case of taking land. The State forces its citizens into the army and compels them to sacrifice their lives in wars which their own conscience condemns. "The State does not allow the holder of

To the "State," however, or to Society in the aggregate, must be accorded the faculty, "right," or power to limit the quantity of land which an individual shall be permitted "to have his own way or to fix his own price."* So, too, the State does not allow "the citizen" to have his own way "when conscience, liberty, and life are at stake;" "nor to fix his own price" for the services he may render or the life he is forced to put in jeopardy.

Yet it must be admitted that in a strictly scientific view of the question, mere occupancy or possession can never give a perfect title to property of any kind. For somebody must have *created* the property by means of labor before anybody could occupy or possess it.

Hence, titles accruing from and originating in occupancy or possession simply, would necessarily involve the overriding and subverting of title based on the production of the values or the property in question, or of such title transferred by sale or gift. All this is incontrovertible, as is also the position that a party can convey no better title than he himself possesses. But does it follow that, inasmuch as these abstract propositions are confessedly true, they can be and should " be embodied in fact," and that society, through the instrumentality of civil government, should undertake their practical assertion? Such an attempt, resolutely persisted in, would speedily unsettle all titles to every species of property, and ultimately plunge society into anarchy and barbarism. The *right* of every man to the property he has in possession would be challengeable, and nobody could feel secure, since it would be very difficult, if not impossible, for one to show that none of the property he possesses has ever changed hands in violation of the abstract propositions above stated. Hence, for reasons mentioned in a preceding page, society has deemed it wise to enact statutes of limitation, making peaceable possession for a specific period competent *legal* evidence that such possession is rightful. Doubtless such statutes sometimes work injustice, and no intelligent man will pretend they may not; but until society reaches absolute perfection, when government will be no longer necessary, they cannot be dispensed with; nor can they be entirely ignored in any scheme for perfecting human institutions and bettering the condition of mankind.

* "The People's Blue Book" for 1872, pp. 444-46.

dividual may own; or in certain extreme cases to override the will of the owner in respect to the management of his estate. The same principle applies to other kinds of property not less forcibly than to property in land. For instance, at this very time,* the people of several of our Western States are profoundly agitated on account of alleged extortions of the great railroad corporations. Suppose that the charge preferred by the farmers is strictly true—that these corporations have so fixed their freight rates as to enable them to make enormous profits on the real cost of their property, while the farmers can make none on theirs. These corporations claim a legal and moral right to charge such rates as they see fit for the use of their own property. Must the farmers, then, be compelled to see their products perish on their hands, or allow all their anticipated profits to be absorbed by the great corporations by means of extortionate freights? Assuming that such abuses exist, society or "the State" should, because individuals cannot, correct them. The same rule and the same reasons are applicable to abuses growing out of land monopoly. Abuses of the latter kind have often been urged as an argument against the private ownership of any portion of the soil; but the same reasoning would

* The Spring of 1873.

be equally pertinent and forcible against the right of private property in railways and in many other forms. State ownership of the soil (secured by the extinguishment of private titles by means of equitable compensation), and a system of leases for definite periods, as proposed by Mr. J. Stuart Mill, if justifiable on the ground that in no other way can the equitable rights of all to the use of this kind of property be effectually secured, would logically tend to a species of communism embracing all kinds of property. The same reasons would justify the same remedy in all cases.

Although it seemed proper to consider very briefly the question of property in land, in order to show that the system of private ownership which prevails in our own and many European countries is, neither in its general features nor in its distinctive principle, altogether wanting in the sanction of natural law; and that accordingly the holders of land have at least a *prima facie* right to the control of the natural forces attaching to their respective possessions; yet the establishment of these propositions is by no means indispensable to the validity of my argument. For whether the ownership of land be vested in the State, or in the "human race," or in individual citizens, the owners, or agents of the owners, would alike desire to devote it to the most profitable uses. The same remarks apply with equal pertinency and force to material property, and the owners of material property, of all other forms and kinds. Whether held by the rightful owner, or by one whose legal title is in fraud of the highest equity, as asserted by Spencer, the holder in either case possesses the faculty of controlling it; and he naturally uses his power of control in the manner which he deems most advantageous to himself.

Without further discussion, it will be assumed that between property in land and property in other material things, there is no such radical difference as to warrant the State or Society in the aggregate in seizing and controlling the former to the absolute exclusion of private ownership, while leaving all forms of the latter kind to be acquired and even monopolized by private persons and corporations without limit or restriction; and that as the laws of science make no radical distinction between the two kinds of property, so the policy of States should be to treat both substantially alike—recognizing and guaranteeing the equitable rights of each, but reserving and exercising the right to intervene in case of flagrant abuses, as well as in cases where obstinacy or private cupidity palpably and unjustly obstructs the promotion of the general welfare.

THE RELATION OF NATURE'S FORCES AND MATERIALS TO VALUE, FURTHER CONSIDERED.

BASTIAT and nearly all recent economical writers hold, as already stated, that value of itself is not a property or quality, or a combination of properties or qualities which may inhere in or attach to any material thing; but that it is simply "a ratio, an external relation"—having reference to "services" exchanged or to be exchanged by or between man and his fellow-man. It hence follows, and they accordingly teach, that there can be no value without exchange, and especially none where there is no opportunity to make exchanges—as in the case of the sack of gold already referred to. They also teach that the materials and forces so liberally supplied by nature cannot possibly constitute, under any conceivable circumstances, even the smallest element of value; that the "utility" which such materials or forces impart to any commodity or product adds nothing to its value; and that it accordingly never affects prices, no matter how many hands a given commodity may pass through, or to how many exchanges it may give rise before it finally reaches the consumer. The gifts of nature, they tell us, are always and necessarily free—whether in the form of materials which enter into the composition of a given product, or of forces by means of which it is wrought into a shape fitted to satisfy the wants of man—free not only to the manufacturer or farmer who uses them in the first instance, but free also and alike under all circumstances and to all mankind.* This latter branch of the general proposition respecting the nature and sources of value, is entitled to some further consideration.

It may be remarked, preliminarily, that the class of economical writers here referred to, concede, or rather assert, the right of property in land as fully as the right of property in other material things; and that ownership vests in the owner of such property the right to the natural forces which appertain to it. Bastiat admits quite as fully that the natural forces—such as man puts in requisition in the work of production—are unequally distributed; but as he frankly declares that his dominant idea is that those who, by superior sagacity or other means, contrive to avail themselves of natural agencies to

---

* See Appendix B for extracts from Bastiat's Works, in which this doctrine is asserted as of universal application.

the greatest possible extent, do not and cannot derive any pecuniary advantage from their co-operation over their fellow-producers who secure far less of nature's aid, he is logically forced to conclude that as the natural forces and materials cost nothing in the first instance, so they can never possess or create value, nor exchange for anything of value, nor impart value to any object whatever. The right of exchange being unobstructed and free, he holds that the materials and forces of nature, being the free gift of God to man, together with all the benefits accruing therefrom, will always be as free to the consumer of a given product as to the manufacturer who produced it: it is human services, and not the gifts of God, that are estimated and exchanged.

And yet he says, "man always seeks conditions which impart most value to his services." He discerns that he may profit by the gifts of God in three ways: 1st, if he takes possession of them himself; or, 2d, if he alone knows the *process* by which they may be utilized; or, 3d, if he possesses the only *instrument* by means of which these gifts may be made to co-operate in the production of values.

Under either of these conditions he gives but *little* of his own labor in exchange for *much* of the labor of others. His services have a large relative value, and one is disposed to believe that such excess of value is inherent in the natural agent.*

It seems strange that having admitted that under the circumstances he describes, and for reasons he sets forth, the fortunate or sagacious man who had secured the most favorable arrangements with nature, would give but little of his own for much of the labor of others, he should not have recognized the true principle underlying all the phenomena of production—that the natural forces constitute one of the indispensable factors in the production of values, and that under varying circumstances they vary largely in efficiency of action—thus producing the precise state of things which he describes. But the "dominant idea" with which he acknowledges he was possessed, prevented his wonderfully acute mind from perceiving it; and he proceeds to argue that the superior value of the product in question resides in the "service" personally rendered by the fortunate or sagacious man, and not at all in "the natural agents, the gifts of God." On a previous page of the same volume he thus assumes to demonstrate that value cannot in any degree accrue from nature, or the action of natural forces.

* This is a rather free translation from Bastiat, Vol. VI., p. 356. The original will be found in Appendix B.

"If value is in matter, it is confounded with the physical qualities of the substance which render them useful to man. But these qualities are often placed there by nature. Then nature concurs in creating *value*, and we attribute value to what is in its essence gratuitous and common. Where then is the basis of property? When the compensation I give to obtain a material product—wheat, for example—is distributed among those who, directly or indirectly, have rendered me *service* in producing it, to whom goes that part of the price which corresponds to the portion of *value* due to nature? To God? Nobody will thus pretend, and nobody has ever seen God claim payment for His services. To man? By what right—since by the hypothesis man did not create it?"*

But this style of argument is by no means conclusive. Indeed if it proves that natural agencies do not assist in creating values, it must necessarily prove also that no human power can create value. For it will not be disputed that Deity is as truly the source of man's mental and muscular powers, as He is of the power which causes seed to germinate and produce its kind. Hence, if He should be paid in case His "services," rendered through the action of

* The original, from Bastiat's complete works, Vol. VI., p. 171, is given in Appendix B.

the natural laws, contribute to the creation of values, He would be equally entitled to share in all values however created, since it is utterly impossible to conceive of any production of values independent of the powers, instrumentalities, and agencies which alike have their origin in the Great First Cause.

Now, the natural forces are said to be free to all mankind; and in one sense they are; that is, to the owner of the matter in which such forces reside, or of the space or territory in which they act—as illustrated in the action of the sun in making salt by evaporation, or in bleaching, etc., etc. To such persons the natural forces, inhering in and limited to such ownership, are free. The owner of land fertilizes it and plants it with corn; and the natural forces reward him with a crop. Had he refrained from planting, the natural forces would have been comparatively dormant or have worked less to his advantage. But whether he plants or refrains from planting, the work done for him by the natural forces is free to him, but to him alone.

So, too, if a man has a fine waterfall on his land—here is a natural force or power which, so long as it is unemployed, does nothing towards producing utilities or values. But the owner of the land on which it is situated is clearly the owner of the waterfall also, and of the power now running to waste. He may build machine shops or mills and use the power for his own benefit; or he may sell it, or hold it for a better price than it will now command. If there is no other waterfall within many miles, he will naturally set his own to work; but why and for whom? Evidently he would not devote his capital and labor to the erection of machinery until he had made up his mind that they would thus produce greater values than they would if otherwise employed—nor if there were the slightest doubt that the values thus produced would be all his own. The natural forces inseparable from the waterfall would operate "gratuitously" for the owner of the surrounding territory who should put them at the work of producing "utilities," and for him only. These forces would perform the work which under other circumstances would necessarily be performed by man—and they would do it cheaper and better, as otherwise they would not supersede muscular power; the "utilities" produced by their agency would possess none the less value because in their production the natural forces had been substituted for manual labor; and the ultimate result would be a given quantity of "utilities" possessing value (inasmuch as they are unobtainable without labor), and costing the producer and owner less than the average cost of like commodities in the local market.

It is unqestionably true, that, even in the hypothetical case under consideration, while the natural forces work primarily and directly for the owner of the water power, they work indirectly and remotely for the benefit of all mankind. In this case there is no other water power within a circle of ten or twenty miles in diameter. The owner of the water power is therefore in no danger of *local* competition; and in the absence of *all* competition, he would naturally sell his products at the highest possible price compatible with the exclusion of the costlier products made by hand. But farther off, indeed at irregular intervals all over the world, there are other waterfalls and machines devoted to the same kind of manufacture, and with these he is obliged to compete. The consequence is a constant tendency towards cheaper production by means of improved machinery and the discovery of new processes, which inures to the benefit of all consumers, or of all mankind. Pending the longer or shorter periods during which the improved machinery and the new processes remain under the exclusive control of the inventor and the discoverer, they alone realize the principal benefit accruing from larger production with the same outlay of capital and labor. But after the expiration of that period, the right to use these means of larger production becomes common to all mankind through all future time. The natural forces which had been utilized more advantageously by the inventor and the discoverer than ever before, and which to that extent had worked almost exclusively for their benefit, henceforth work for all on equal terms. Or, in the words of Bastiat, their co-operation with human labor is henceforth "gratuitous;" and the consumers of the commodities, the production of which had thus been increased and cheapened, are benefited in proportion to the resulting fall in prices.

But it would be a great mistake, hence, to conclude that the time will ever come when all "natural advantages" will "become under the law of competition, the common and *gratuitous* patrimony of consumers, of society, of mankind."* For although inventions by means of which the natural forces are rendered more efficient in the work of production, and which are to-day private property, will to-morrow "become the common and gratuitous patrimony of mankind;" they will be succeeded by other inventions which for a certain period will also be private property; and these later inventions will enable their owners to utilize the natural forces to

* White's "Bastiat," p. 55.

better advantage than the rest of mankind and consequently to their own profit, until these in their turn become "common and gratuitous." Such substantially has been the course of events for centuries; and it is quite safe to assume that it is not destined to change for centuries to come. And, assuming that the notions of value and the production of values here advocated are correct, it is perfectly obvious that meanwhile the forces of Nature will, under certain circumstances, constitute a factor in the production of values; and that they can never be altogether "the common and gratuitous patrimony of mankind."

But lest it should for a moment be supposed that the correctness of the notions of value and production above referred to, is entirely dependent upon the correctness of the assumption of the continuance of invention and discovery, which for a time places a certain class at an advantage with respect to all other classes, it may be proper to remark again in this connection, that so long as there are mines of unequal richness, lands óf unequal fertility, and a thousand other industries presenting the same general aspects, just so long we shall be obliged to contemplate the phenomena of unequal values accruing from equal sums of labor—all other aids and accessories of production being the same excepting only the single element or factor, the forces and materials supplied by nature.

There is a tract of land in this immediate neighborhood* where, in the short distance of twenty or thirty yards, one may pass from a sandy soil, that is naturally sterile, to a clayey soil, originally overlaid with a rich vegetable mold or muck. This sharp line of demarcation between these two kinds of soil extends for a considerable distance. The land on either side of the line was cleared of the native forest at about the same time, and it is of my own personal knowledge that for years afterwards the clay land could be as safely relied on for over two tons of hay to the acre, as could the sandy land for one-half a ton. The labor required for the richer land did not exceed that which the sandy land required, excepting only the slight difference which the harvesting of the larger crop of the richer land rendered necessary. The original cost of these two varieties of soil to the State was nominal: and they were sold to the first occupiers at precisely the same price. Here then is a case where, with the insignificant difference above noted, a given amount of labor and capital expended on the richer, yielded at least four times as much hay as the same amount of labor and capital expended on the poorer soil. Now it would seem to

* Lot No. 40 in the town of Irondequoit, New York.

be so clear as to admit of no question whatever, that the larger product was due solely to the greater intensity, abundance or efficiency of the natural forces inherent in the clayey soil; for taking the facts as they existed, the only elements of production which were not alike in quality and amount or efficiency in respect to the two kinds of soil, were those which nature supplied. Another fact remains to be stated. The hay grown on the clayey soil was worth fully as much per ton as that grown on the sandy soil. Hence the conclusion, that in this case the larger product and the greater value were due to the more efficient action of the natural forces, or to their more favorable co-operation with the capital and the labor of man.

It is very obvious that the principles involved in this case are of wide, if not indeed of universal application. Were the two kinds of soil separated by miles or hundreds of miles instead of a few yards merely, the same principles would apply, the same practical results would follow, and they would warrant precisely the same conclusion. So too, if several soils of nearly equal fertility, the respective products of which under given conditions would vary in quantity and value from five to fifteen per cent. only, be substituted for the two above described, the same principles would apply, and they would have the same bearing upon the scientific question under consideration.

Instead of the new lands of America, let us take two tracts of equal area in Great Britain, one of which, belonging to A., is naturally sterile and barely produces enough to pay for the labor expended upon it and prevent its abandonment by the owner; while the other, belonging to B., is naturally fertile, and yields a product of four times greater value, the cost of labor being substantially the same as paid by A. Both tracts were originally "gratuitous," and cost the first owners nothing. B.'s land has always paid him or his predecessors a handsome return in excess of the cost of working it, while A.'s has never paid but little more than he has expended upon it. At the present time B.'s land will sell for a much larger sum than A.'s. If the work performed by nature is always "gratuitous"—not only to him for whom it is done in the first instance, but to everybody and "throughout all human transactions," and hence can never give rise to, or constitute an element of, value—if such is the fact, how can the difference in favor of B. be accounted for? An account embracing both A.'s and B.'s property from "the beginning" would show that B.'s now stands him in much less than A.'s; yet it is worth much more, and will readily sell or exchange for a much larger sum of money or other values. This case, though hypothetical, contains no challengeable feature; and in respect to principles involved, it is in strict harmony with facts familiar to all. Its solution is impossible so long as the "dominant idea" is adhered to. But it is readily solved if the respective farms of A. and B. are regarded as belonging in the same category as machines or other agencies of production. B.'s is better, because more effective than A.'s; with the same quantity of labor it will yield a larger product of standard quality, and consequently it will afford its owner a larger profit. A farm or machine vests in its owner the exclusive use of the natural forces attaching thereto; and since they are more efficient in B.'s farm than they are in A.'s, a given quantity of labor in either case being assumed, his farm is correspondingly the more valuable.

As the dominant idea of Bastiat confessedly is, that while "nature and man must concur in every article of production, the portion of nature is always gratuitous," * he reiterates it in different phraseology in most of his essays on the production or distribution of values, and sustains it with a great variety of arguments and illustrations. This will perhaps justify a reiteration of argument and illustration of opposite tenor. He says, "the exchanges of com-

* White's "Translation of Bastiat's Essays," p. 51.

merce are between labor and labor." "Traffic is an exchange of values." "Traffic is the exchange of equal labors." "Only so much of the usefulness of an article as is the result of human labor becomes the object of mutual exchange, and consequently of remuneration. The remuneration varies much no doubt, in proportion to the intensity of the labor, of the skill which it requires, of its being *apropos* to the demand of the day, of the need which exists for it, of the momentary absence of competition, etc. But it is not the less true in principle that the assistance received from natural laws, which belongs to all, counts for nothing in the price." *

He admits that "competition establishes for each category [of products] a price current," and the proposition hitherto stated † will not be controverted, that the price of *each* standard product approximates the average cost of all.

Now suppose—the hypothesis being substantially in accord with many known facts—suppose a man engaged in gold washing on a river bottom realizes from his own labor, by means of a very rude apparatus, ten dollars a day in gold dust; while another man, equally "skilled" and laboring with equal "intensity," who is working a claim but a short

* White's Translation of "Bastiat's Essays," pp. 51, 55, 56.
† See page 48 of this work.

distance away, can get only enough of the precious dust to amount to two dollars a day. If "traffic is the exchange of equal labor," and "the portion of nature is always gratuitous," on what basis can the respective products of these two days' labor be exchanged for each other, or for other products of known value? It is well known that many of the large gold, silver and quicksilver mining companies of the Pacific States and Territories, exhibit discrepancies in their financial results, quite as great as that of the above hypothesis. They range all the way from ruinous deficits to annual profits of hundreds per cent. upon the capital originally invested. It is quite certain that the owners of these various properties are all animated by one purpose—to get the largest possible return for their capital and their labor; and that their "skill" and the "intensity" of their labor do not vary to any appreciable extent —certainly not to such an extent as to account for the widely different results. How then is it possible, on the principle so positively asserted by Bastiat, to account for the widely differing values accruing from the same amounts of labor devoted with like "intensity" to the production of values? For it should not for a moment be forgotten that he holds that "the forces and *the materials* given by God gratuitously to man in the beginning, have remained, are still, and will ever be, gratuitous, throughout all human transactions; for in the valuations to which exchanges give rise, it is *human services* and NOT *the gifts of God* which are mutually valued and exchanged." *

In the cases under consideration, all the elements supplied by man are the same, but the "materials," which are "the gifts of God," as between the enterprises subjected to comparison, differ widely; and the resulting values produced differ in the same proportion. It should not, indeed it could not, be so, were the "dominant idea" of Bastiat correct; for if "human services" only are valued and compensated in exchanging the products of human industry, and the "materials and forces of nature" "count for nothing in the price," the resulting values in these enterprises would necessarily be strictly proportional to the labor employed—the other accessories of production being the same in all.

Let us make still further application of the doctrine and the principles under consideration, to agriculture, one of the largest and most general, as mining for the precious metals is one of the most limited industries of civilized man. For this purpose let us take a broad expanse of country, the soil of which is generally fertile, the climatic conditions substantially

* Bastiat's " Complete Works," Vol. VI., p. 297.

alike, though not uniform, and the cultivators intelligent, industrious and frugal. In all large tracts of country there is more or less diversity in the natural qualities of the soil, the lay of the land with respect to the sun, natural irrigation, etc. Some of it has a southern and some a northern exposure; some of it is on the hill-top and some in the valley; and some of it is more and some less retentive of the moisture supplied by dew and rain. The respective owners of the different qualities of soil are well aware that certain products require more and others less of heat and moisture; and that some will flourish on a comparatively poor soil, while others require a soil of great natural richness, or one that has been artificially fertilized. They accordingly plant their crops with reference to these known facts, basing their calculations on the ordinary or average amount of heat and moisture annually supplied by nature to their respective localities.

Now it is a well-established fact that taking long and definite periods as the basis of comparison, the amount of precipitation and of natural heat respectively, is almost exactly the same in any given tract of country. It is an equally well established fact, that taking single years, and especially the portions of the year during which crops grow and ripen as the basis of comparison, and limiting it to a given locality, rain-fall and natural heat are so wide in their range of variation that in one year or portion of a year, they may be in quantity just what is necessary to the greatest possible production, or they may be so excessive or so scant, as to be absolutely destructive; and they may fluctuate from year to year, between the two extremes indicated, sometimes enabling the cultivator to realize only a moderate profit on his capital and labor; but sometimes also subjecting him to considerable loss. It will be understood as a part of the hypothesis, that the labor employed is the same, whether nature does or does not favor the cultivator, excepting only the variation incident to harvesting a scanty or an abundant crop; yet as a matter of fact, the cultivator often expends more labor when nature is unpropitious, in trying to counteract the effects of excessive heat or cold, or moisture, and is still obliged to accept a smaller compensation than less labor would have yielded under more favorable natural auspices. Here then we have the same result as already noted—a large discrepancy in values produced by different cultivators, each of whom gave employment to the same amount and kind of labor. The constant and unvarying element in these cases is labor, supplemented and assisted in each respectively, by a given amount of capital; the inconstant and varying one is supplied by nature, and the result is values corresponding more or less nearly to the variations of that one element.

Let us consider the facts embodied in this hypothesis, in another aspect: Some crops require more, others less heat and moisture. One farmer in a given year plants very largely the former, and his neighbor as largely, the latter class. The season is an extreme one as regards heat and moisture; the unfortunate farmer vainly puts forth all his energy and skill to neutralize its damaging effects upon his growing crops, but he scarcely harvests as much as the seed he had sown; while the fortunate one, with less than the average labor, secures a most abundant harvest. Again, take the case of other two farmers, and suppose that instead of planting different crops, each plants the same—one on ground requiring much, the other on ground requiring little heat and moisture to produce abundantly. The season being an extreme one, the unfortunate farmer gets for his labor but a small return, while his more fortunate neighbor, who has expended no more labor, gets a large crop. The product in the two cases being of the same kind and quality, sells for the same price by the pound or bushel; and the consequence is, that the values accruing to the two farmers respectively, each exerting or employing the same labor, differ in exact proportion to the weight or measure of their material products, less perhaps by a part of the cost incident to harvesting and marketing the larger product.

Now if the materials and forces supplied by nature are always free throughout all the processes of production and all commercial transactions, and if the product of labor (freedom of exchange being understood) always exchanges for the product of equal labor, the ultimate result in the above hypothesis would inevitably be different. For suppose the unfortunate farmer, A., obtained only thirty bushels of wheat, while the fortunate farmer, B., obtained one hundred bushels for the same labor, on the free natural force and agency theory, A. would be entitled to demand of B. one hundred bushels of wheat in exchange for his thirty bushels; or at least to demand an equal division of their combined product.

It can hardly be alleged with seriousness, that the fortunate man in the several foregoing hypotheses may have been rewarded with greater values because of, and in proportion to, his superior sagacity and skill—the former enabling him to foretell and the latter to profit by the foreseen peculiarities of ever-varying climates. For notwithstanding the recent wonderful achievements in the science of meteorology, the wisest of those who have made it the study of their lives will not pretend that they can forecast the seasons with such accuracy and so long in advance, as to supply the farmer with a safe practical guide for his industrial operations. Moreover, on the always free natural force and material theory, the sagacious man would have little interest in seeking the co-operation of nature under such conditions as would result in the largest possible sum of products and "utilities" from his own labor; since on that theory these products and "utilities" could be obtained in exchange for a lesser sum of both by the man who had been less fortunate in securing nature's aid. For it is labor for labor as embodied in different products that is the basis of exchange, according to the theory under consideration; and the varying degrees in which nature assists or has been supposed to assist in the work of producing values, can under no circumstances give rise to varying values so long as the labor employed is a fixed or given sum in all the cases subjected to comparison.

However the respective partisans of opposing theories may endeavor to account for the fact, the fact itself will be disputed by none, that there is a constant stream of emigration, composed mainly of the poor, the hardy and the enterprising, from the thickly-peopled portions of Europe to the sparsely-peopled regions of America, Australia, and the Pacific Islands. It is a fact equally indisputable, that in those thinly-peopled countries the settlers generally are able to produce, not only more of *useful* things, but things possessing more *value* and commanding a larger sum of "utilities" and values by free exchange in the commercial centres of the world, than they could produce in the countries whence they came. It is well known that a small portion of the mass of emigrants leave their own country with the avowed purpose of making a fortune in "the States" or in "the Colonies," and then returning to enjoy it in the land of their birth; and it is also known that while some fail in their efforts, some also succeed.

All these facts seem to me to prove beyond question that the element in the production of values, composed of the materials and forces of nature, is "remunerated" to the advantage of him whom they primarily serve, instead of being "free to all throughout all human transactions."

In the early days of gold-mining in California, the wages of labor were from five to ten times higher than the same labor would command in Europe or the Atlantic States; and money was let at more than fifty per cent. per annum. And yet men paid these high rates for capital and labor and made large profits. The only explanation the fact admits of is simply this: the unappropriated raw materials of nature in the form of gold-dust mixed with the alluvium of the river bottoms, were so exceptionally abundant that one day's rude labor, would produce more gold than would suffice to pay, perhaps, twenty days' labor in an agricultural country. Here then, clearly, labor was a smaller, and the materials of nature a larger and more efficient element in producing values, than they respectively constitute in the ordinary processes of production.

This industry may be worthy of a little further remark. In its earlier days the miners were few in number; they could select portions of alluvial soil that were the richest in gold deposits for the field of their operations, and appropriate to their exclusive use the entire proceeds of their labor. Presently, however, this state of things is altogether changed. Instead of being practically free to all, the whole area of gold-bearing territory has become the acknowledged property of a large number of owners, every one of whom asserts his proprietary rights in respect to gold quite as jealously and as efficiently as in respect to timber or other vegetable growths. Meanwhile, persons have been attracted to the gold-fields from all parts of the world, and the number of miners has been quadrupled. Hence there is, in the first instance, only one-fourth of the quantity of gold lands per man that there was originally; but this one-fourth has become the property of private owners, of whom the miner, if not himself a landowner, must buy the privilege of prosecuting his peculiar industry before he can earn one dollar. The favors of nature, which at first (whether rightfully or not) were practically free to all, have now been appropriated and divided and subdivided, until they are only, say, one-fourth the original amount per man; and that smaller portion must be still further diminished by the royalty or other form of charge demanded by the owner of the land for the privilege of mining on his private property. It is perfectly obvious that under this altered state of things the average weight of gold produced by each man will be less than it was when the miners were only one-fourth their present number; and it is equally obvious that the present gold product will exchange for other gold, or for values in any other form, on the *basis of weight* (standard fineness being implied), and not on the basis of the ever-varying quantities of *labor* employed in producing the various lots of gold of given weight. In these several hypotheses, the constant and unchanging element is labor—equal skill and application being assumed in all cases; the gifts of nature supply the inconstant and changeable one, and the result is equal labor produces unequal values. It is worthy of mention that the rights accruing from private property in land come in as a disturbing force in the partition and distribution of the materials and forces of nature; but it will be borne in mind that throughout the whole field of economical science, almost every material thing, including land, has its acknowledged owner, whose consent must be obtained by purchase or otherwise, as a condition precedent to its being used by other parties for their own purposes.

But if an agricultural district be substituted for a gold-bearing one, the same general principles will apply, and conduct to the same conclusion. Suppose a million of people occupy a given territory, all of which has been parcelled out into farms and brought to a high state of cultivation by the respective owners. Suppose further, that all at once another million of people migrate to the territory and buy one-half the land of the former owners. We should now have twice as many farms and twice as much labor as formerly, but the quantity of land would remain the same. In other words, the sum of labor available for production would be doubled, but the gifts of nature would not be increased. No argument can be necessary to convince the intelligent and candid reader that the doubling of the labor element, under the circumstances, would not effect a doubling of the values produced. One of the elements or factors in the case supposed has not been increased or raised; but if the hypothesis admitted the raising of this factor in the same ratio as the other, the result would clearly be an increase of values produced in the same proportion—it being assumed, of course, that the requisite capital and other accessories of production should hold the same relation in either case.

Unquestionably it may be alleged that the hypothesis includes features that could not possibly be realized—that the halving of farms and the doubling of cultivators throughout a large territory can never take place simultaneously. The fact will be readily admitted. But the admission of this fact does not in the least degree impair the force of the reasoning. For it will not be disputed that in thinly-peopled agricultural districts, where the land is owned by the cultivators and its transfer is not obstructed by law, farms are subdivided and sold in parcels to immigrants and to the landless sons of the resident owners. Thus, by natural processes well known to all, farms are multiplied in number, their average area is correspondingly diminished, and the sum of labor is increased in the same ratio. But whether the increase in the number of farms and laborers respectively is one hundred per cent. or only ten per cent., and whether it should take place in a single day or require a century for its accomplishment, the principles involved would be the same, and the arguments deducible therefrom would lose none of their pertinency or force. The simultaneous changes in numbers and conditions assumed in the hypothesis, if not possible, are certainly thinkable. Considered as taking place slowly and requiring a long period for their actual realization, it would be extremely difficult to measure their practical effect in altering the relation between a given amount of labor and the sum of values it produces, under the respective conditions of the hypothesis. Any estimate of the net effect of such changes, based on a comparison of values produced at the beginning with those produced at the end of a long period, is liable to be complicated with the effects of improved processes of production, with the influence on nominal values accruing from variations in the monetary standard, from special legislation, etc., etc. But by putting the proposition in the abstract, as it is stated in the hypothesis, the mind is left free to consider the main question unembarrassed by the presence of variable collateral agencies affecting the sum of values which given quantities of labor would produce under the conditions respectively described. These agencies, introduced as a distinct element in the problem to be solved, may mislead the judgment; and they may also obscure, but under no circumstances can they possibly change, the action of the natural laws.

RE-STATEMENT AND APPLICATION OF PRINCIPLES.

The following propositions will henceforth be considered as established:—

1st. That value is a real entity and not "merely an external relation" between fictitious or unreal things, the very existence of which is denied by those who thus define it.

2d. That the only elements or factors that are indispensable to the production of value, and into which all values are resolvable, are human labor and the materials and forces of nature.

3d. That the relative efficiency of these elements or factors in the work of production, instead of being fixed and constant, is fluctuating and variable; that hence given quantities of labor, in a multitude of cases, will produce different values, assuming that skill, capital, and all other accessories of production are the same in every case; and that the only difference between the various cases consists in the more or less efficient co-operation of the natural forces.

4th. That land and other material things being subject to appropriation and ownership as private property, the natural forces pertaining thereto may be used "gratuitously" by the owner of the property to which they pertain, like machinery or any other agency of production, and the resulting product belongs to him alone.

Now every piece or parcel of property of whatever kind, existing in a country, has its owner, who is entitled to its exclusive use, except as against the State under certain conditions. So, too, all labor has its owners—that is, in the first instance, the persons who labor.

Hence it will be observed that the natural forces which are utilized in the work of production, and which are one of its indispensable factors, act exclusively through or upon material media—and these in civilized countries are all appropriated and owned as private property; and that labor, the other indispensable element or factor in the work of production, in all free countries belongs to the persons who

labor, and is subject to their exclusive control.
Thus both of the elements or factors through whose
joint action alone wealth or value is produced, are
really or virtually the private property of individuals. The same may be said of all the intelligence,
capital, credit, skill, and other aids and accessories
of production included within the territorial limits
of any country.

Economical science always assumes that every
owner of any of these factors, elements, or accessories of production is at all times desirous of using
them in such a manner as will prove most advantageous to himself.*

All the elements, materials, and forces which
enter into and contribute to the production of value
or wealth, are now before us. It would seem to be
perfectly clear, that, prompted by self-interest and
guided by the best judgment he can form after due
reflection—and consultation, if he sees fit to consult
others—every man who has labor to dispose of,
whether original or employed, will aim to secure
such co-operation of the natural forces as will yield
him in excess of cost the largest, *i. e.*, the most valuable product. It would seem to be equally clear

---

* The intelligent economist does not need to be reminded that political economy takes no cognizance of charities or gifts of any kind, regarding them as outside of its domain.

that every man possessing disposable capital, or who owns a "property" consisting in the right of control over the productive agencies of nature, will also aim to secure such co-operation or arrangement with labor—directly or indirectly—as will yield him the largest or most valuable net return. These propositions, it is believed, include in their scope every factor, element, and auxiliary of production.

In all this discussion, thus far, it is implied or assumed that man, the thinking and directing factor in the work of production, is neither controlled nor embarrassed by the direct or indirect intervention of the government, but that he is left free to devote his capital, his intelligence, and his labor to such industries as in his judgment will pay him best. It is but a modified statement of a preceding proposition to say that, under these circumstances, all the natural advantages of a country, as discerned and recognized by its people, who respectively possess the right of control over or of "property" in them, will be devoted to the most profitable uses in so far as possible—the limitation being indicated by the sums of capital, labor, and intelligence, respectively available for the work of production.

The result would necessarily be the largest yearly aggregate of profits or net values which could accrue to a given country, from an intelligent and interested direction of all its factors, agencies, and forces of production.*

* It is an obvious corollary from the above, that the aggregate annual production of values in a given country cannot *exceed* the sum which its elements, accessories, and forces would produce were they all put in requisition by the highest conceivable intelligence and to the best possible advantage. It is equally obvious that the labor of a given country, together with its available capital, and all other accessories of production, will, under the direction of the best intelligence the country affords for that purpose, seek for and make such arrangements for the co-operation of the natural forces as, in the judgment of the directing authority, will result in the largest possible production of values. This latter sum will naturally increase with (even if not in proportion to) the growth of intelligence, the invention of new machinery, and the discovery of improved processes of production; but it is *probable* there will always remain a large but incalculable difference between this sum and the *possible* aggregate of annual values above indicated. It may also be remarked, in this connection, as an obvious fact, that any legislation—such, for instance, as the levying of import duties—must necessarily, to some extent, divert labor and capital from such arrangements for the co-operation of nature as had been made with reference to the largest possible gains, substitute less advantageous arrangements in their stead, and cause a diminution of aggregate values annually produced.

NATURAL INDICATIONS AS TO THE EMPLOYMENT OF CAPITAL AND LABOR.

H. C. Carey has written several volumes in which he aims to prove that nature correctly indicates the kinds of industry to which a people should devote their energies. He has accordingly proved, to his own satisfaction, as also to the satisfaction of many of his countrymen—especially of such as are manufacturing commodities requiring or desiring protection—that inasmuch as our country is the great producer of cotton, and as we have mines of iron ore and coal in great abundance, therefore nature has clearly indicated that the cotton-mill should long ago have been placed in the cotton-growing region, and iron furnaces and rolling-mills should have been constructed in order to produce all the iron the country needs, instead of importing it or any portion of it from abroad. But he holds that Great Britain, by the vast and cheap production of iron and cotton goods, has rendered the realization of this natural order of things at present impossible; and that high duties, reaching the prohibitive point, if necessary, must be imposed in order to prevent British interference with our home industries, and enable our people to place the furnace and the cotton-mill in their natural position, beside the cotton-field and the iron-mine. Horace Greeley, too, while strenuously advocating protection, admits that commerce performs a "beneficial function" in the interchange of the "natural products" of various countries, "so that all may enjoy, in a measure, the blessings divinely bestowed upon each." "Show me," he continues, "that *nature* has interposed a serious barrier to the growth or production of any staple in my country, and I will strenuously insist that no duty be imposed on the importation of that product, unless for revenue." 'I do not propose a contravention of the laws of nature, nor of any of them." *

The substance of all this is, that the indications of nature—using the term in a broad sense—are the safest and the proper guides in respect to the industries man should pursue in any given locality, and that the careful and intelligent observer need not be at fault on this subject. This position is eminently sound and correct. The natural laws never furnish a wrong or unsafe rule of action. But in referring a question to the natural laws for solution,

* Greeley's "Political Economy, Art, Commerce, and Exchanges."

great care should be taken to present for consideration *all* the elements of the problem to be solved. The neglect of this essential condition is the fruitful source of erroneous conclusions on the part of the advocates of protective duties. For instance, Greeley teaches that the iron, cotton, and woollen manufacturers of this country should be stimulated by means of protection, because there is no "serious obstacle" in the way, nor is such a policy "a contravention of the laws of nature nor of any one of them." How is this conclusion reached? Simply by contemplating the fact that iron ore and coal are found in close proximity in some localities, and the cotton-fields, abundant water-power, and "cheap labor" in others. Hence he concludes that there is no "serious barrier to the production" of iron and cotton goods in this country, and they should therefore be protected against foreign competition. But the real question is *not* whether there exists a "serious barrier" to the *making* of iron and cotton goods, but whether they can be made here (to the extent he desires) at a *greater profit* than can be realized from other industries? To this question the fact that the material elements of these products are found in close proximity, does not of itself warrant an affirmative reply. The controlling motive of man in all industrial undertakings is, not to produce certain commodities, but to make profits. Thus it will be observed the manufacture of iron or cotton is not the real end at which he is aiming; it may be the best way to reach that end, but it also may not be. The question remains, is it the best way or is it not? and on that question the proximity of iron and coal, of cotton and water power, reflects none but an uncertain and deceptive light—as will be seen by a few practical illustrations.

Here are iron ore and coal, lying side by side, and close at hand are fertile soils. Protectionism says, Nature indicates that iron *should* be made *here* instead of getting it from a distance—especially instead of importing it from abroad. But the intelligent laborer or capitalist responds, Iron cannot be made here as cheaply as it can be imported. Then says protectionism, Let us have an import duty so heavy that you can *make* iron cheaper than you can import it.

But, says the intelligent capitalist or laborer, Nature indicates, by the very presence of fertile soils, by the cultivation and exchange of the products of which iron can be imported cheaper than it can be made here,—nature thus indicates that our true way to get iron is to buy it and pay for it in agricultural products. We can thus get, delivered here, a ton of iron for less labor than we can by making it. Nature does not speak through iron and coal mines only, but she speaks just as clearly and authoritatively to man by pointing him to fertile soils, from which he can realize more "utilities" and more values, by the expenditure of equal labor and capital, than he can from the mines of coal and iron.

Again, let the hypothesis be amended, and suppose the alluvium of the valleys in the coal and iron region is rich in gold, which may be readily separated by means of a very primitive apparatus. So long as all available labor and capital could find full employment in gold-washing and make extraordinary profits, nobody would advise the abandonment or the neglect of that industry for the purpose of embarking in the manufacture of iron. The iron and coal are right here, alongside of the gold-bearing soil; a ton of iron could be produced here with as little labor as in England; but the same labor that would produce the ton of American iron would produce enough gold to pay for a ton and a half of English iron, delivered in the American iron region. Of course, so long as this state of facts should last, no labor and capital would be devoted to iron-making in that locality—for the simple reason that they could find more profitable employment in the gold-field, where nature offers more favorable terms of co-operation. Change the hypothesis again, and instead of placing the gold-field alongside the iron and coal, place it at any distance from them, provided it is still accessible to the same labor and capital as the iron region. It is obvious that labor and capital would still go to the gold region in preference to staying at home and making iron at a much smaller profit. Once more change the hypothesis, and let its conditions be iron ore and coal in close proximity, and soils of varying fertility distributed all over the country, from one mile to a thousand miles distant from the iron region. Under these circumstances capital and labor would do precisely the same as it is assumed they would do under the above hypothesis and as they do now—that is, they would carefully inquire in what industry nature would aid them most in producing values, and they would be controlled in their action by the result of their inquiries—some doubtless selecting agriculture as their occupation, some iron-making, and some various other industries, according as each individual should deem one or the other best suited to his own tastes and qualifications, and best calculated to yield him a large compensation for his capital or labor.

CLAIMS OF PROTECTIONISM.

The advocates of "protection to home industry" by means of duties levied upon imports, claim that it causes a "diversity of pursuits," "renders human labor more effective—that is, more productive," and "increases individual, national and general wealth." *
As "diversity of pursuits" is not necessarily a benefit to a people, as will presently appear, the main question is, does protection by the means indicated, or by any other means, render the labor of a country *generally*, or in the aggregate, "more productive," and thus "increase individual, national and general wealth?"

It is unquestionably true that if the conditions of the largest possible production are correctly described in the foregoing pages, then any departure from those conditions, such as protection requires, must necessarily have the effect of diminishing production; and any further argument might well be dispensed with. But it may not be amiss to consider somewhat in detail, and by a slight variation of method, the pretensions and arguments of those who advocate protective duties as a most efficient means

* See "Protection Explained," by Horace Greeley.

of "increasing individual, national and general wealth."

DIVERSIFICATION OF INDUSTRY.

One of the favorite arguments of the protectionists, is, that protection causes "a diversity of pursuits," and hence furnishes additional employment to labor and "increases the general wealth." That it does compel capital and labor to abandon old "pursuits" and seek new ones, must be conceded; for in no other way could it make itself sensibly felt. But to allege that this compulsion is a benefit to the capital and labor of a country as a whole, and that it tends to increase individual and national wealth, is simply to beg the question at issue. Following Greeley's example, let us take Iowa as a type of the whole country; assume that there are no duties on imports, and that her people get their clothing by raising wheat, and exchanging it for British goods. Now it will be borne in mind that at any given time, the labor and the natural forces—the indispensable elements or factors of production—as also the capital, intelligence, and all accessories of production, are respectively fixed and definite, though not precisely ascertainable quantities. The desire to make the most profitable use of all the forces and agencies of production being always assumed to be present and active in every person engaged in the work of producing values, this state of facts must always exist at any given time; every person (*i. e.*, all persons in the country) devoting his energies and his means to productive industry, is using such energies and means of production in such manner as in his judgment will yield him the largest profits. In the case under consideration he is applying them to the raising of wheat for a foreign market; because after the most careful and intelligent calculation he can make, he concludes that that industry will pay him best, and necessarily add most to individual and national wealth. But it may be said "he errs in judgment; he is mistaken in his calculations; the aggregate wealth *would* be largely increased by a diversification of industry—which protection alone can effect." *

* Many people of intelligence are undoubtedly imposed upon by the persistent representations of the protectionists that under an absolute free-trade policy there would be no such thing as a general diversity of pursuits. But a little reflection could hardly fail to convince any one of that class that in a country possessing so great diversity of soil, climate, minerals, etc., and inhabited by a people of such varied tastes, aptitudes and acquirements, and of so much intelligence and enterprise as ours, there would be a great diversity of pursuits under any conceivable policy on the part of the government. The fact mentioned on a preceding page (21) that iron was made in this country 200 years ago, when the mother country, so far from protecting, endeavored to discourage its manufacture; and that it steadily increased through every subsequent decade whatever policy prevailed, would seem to be sufficient proof of this prop-

This is simply assertion—the opinion of a theorist in opposition to the judgment of a man vitally interested in the practical solution of the question and intelligently comparing the results of various industries. Again; the several factors, elements and accessories of production being respectively at any given time, fixed and definite quantities, it would appear to be absolutely necessary to increase the quantity or the activity of some or all these factors and forces, in order to increase the sum of values resulting from their joint action or co-operation in the work of production. It will not be pretended that all or any one of these factors and forces can be *increased* directly and arbitrarily by legislative enactment. In other words, a law levying protective duties does not of itself add to the

osition. For the iron manufacture is one which it is claimed would be utterly ruined by the withdrawal of protection. Indeed H. C. Carey goes so far as to allege (see his " Harmony of Interests," p. 132) that the adoption of free trade by the United States *" would close every furnace and rolling-mill, and every cotton and woollen factory in the country."* Were this allegation true—as every man of sound sense and ordinary intelligence knows it is not—it would furnish a very strange reason for the continuance of protective duties. Carey presents all these industries as utterly dependent on the charity of others; or on their own ability to *take* a portion of the fruits of other industries in spite of all remonstrance or opposition on the part of the forced contributors. That such is the attitude of his favorite industries, according to his own representation, is none the less true because he argues that to plunder other industries by means of his " system," is only a mode of forcing upon them the greatest possible benefits.

number of laborers, nor to the amount of capital, nor to the sum of the natural forces, nor to the skill, powers of endurance and general intelligence of the people. There remains, then, no mode by which protective duties could effect an increase in the sum of values produced, except that of stimulating to greater activity and efficiency some or all of the elements, factors and forces above mentioned.

It must be remembered that only one of the indispensable elements or factors of production is endowed with the faculty of thinking and willing, and is swayed by moral considerations and by appetites and passions. The other—including in the remark all aids and accessories—is passive, inanimate and unreasoning. Any stimulant designed to give increased activity to the action of the elements or factors of production, must therefore be addressed to that element or *partner* in the work which thinks, feels and wills—to labor, to man.

Now the only way to stimulate labor is to *increase its reward*. Let us see whether a protective tariff is competent for this purpose; that is, to increase the sum of net values annually produced—the elements and forces of production, of course, remaining the same.

Reverting to the typical case already cited, it will be noted that under free trade the labor of the country, or so much of it as was necessary to supply the people with clothing, was devoted to raising wheat to be exchanged for British goods of the kind desired. Protectionism says to this class of labor, or to capitalists who employ it, "Why send to Britain for cloth? You have a country well adapted to sheep-raising; you have water power and labor—all the materials and conditions for making cloth here at home. Why not place the factory among the consumers and save the cost of transporting your grain to Britain, and British goods thence to Iowa?" The capitalist—who may be taken as the representative of intelligent labor—after going over his estimates and calculations anew, says to protectionism, "My figures show conclusively, and I can demonstrate to you, that if I invest fifty or a hundred thousand dollars in a woollen factory I cannot place cloth of my own making in the market at as low a price as I can buy British cloth of the same quality. The inevitable result of such an enterprise would be, the merchants of the neighborhood would undersell me, and my investment in woollen manufacture would prove a total loss." "Well," protectionism rejoins, "it would seem that you are right; you cannot *now* afford to pay men to work in a woollen mill as much as they can earn by raising grain. But all this must be changed—the waste occasioned by this double transportation must be prevented. I will get Congress to enact a protective tariff and will then see you again."

Looking at the same community after the lapse of years, a great change is observable. Congress has been induced to pass a tariff act which protects cloth to the extent, say, of forty per cent. The capitalist has built a woollen mill and it is in successful operation. A thriving little village has grown up around the factory; and "the distance which separates the farms from the manufactories" has been "shortened," "thereby diminishing the [too] heavy cost of exchanging their products respectively." But let us inquire how this great change has been effected, in order to determine whether it is beneficial to the people in the aggregate—whether it has increased the "national and general wealth." To recapitulate a little, it is clear that the protective tariff has not added a single one to the number of people who labor—since Congress does not possess the creative power; nor has it added to the existing capital of the country, nor to the materials and forces which nature supplies. It necessarily follows that it has simply driven a portion of capital and labor from certain industries and induced them to engage in certain other industries; and that is all. And how was this done?

Prior to the passage of the tariff, the people, according to the hypothesis, procured their clothing by raising grain and exchanging it for British goods. Land was so cheap, the soil so fertile and the climate so favorable—in other words, nature was so liberal in proffering her co-operation to the grain-grower, that the citizen could obtain clothing, as also many other articles he required, at a less cost by raising wheat and exchanging it for them, than he could in any other way. The cost of these articles to himself, of course, included freight and all other charges; but still it was so small that nobody could produce them in his grain-producing country, unless the government should interfere to encourage that particular industry at the expense of others. The imposition of a forty per cent. tax on all imported cloths, however, had wrought a change. The importation of cloth had substantially stopped the moment the high duty took effect, because the intelligent capitalists knew that cloth could be made in the country at a profit as soon as foreign cloth should be subjected to forty per cent. duty and various other charges; they had prepared to supply the "home market" with cloths of "home manufacture." The foreign market for the wheat hitherto exported in exchange for cloth, was virtually closed by our ceasing to purchase cloth in return.* The "home market" for wheat was

* This is not intended to be literally exact, but simply to convey

depressed somewhat in proportion to the limitation of the area of sale by the passage of the protective tariff. For the number to be fed at home was the same as before; and the foreign demand was much impaired. This falling off in the demand for wheat and the forty per cent. protection on cloths, necessarily diverted both capital and labor from agriculture to manufactures. That was the design of protection; and had the price of grain not fallen, the forty per cent. bounty or protection would doubtless have sufficed.

Here it may be remarked that the same intelligence, capital and labor which under the "stimulus" of a forty per cent. protection had embarked in cloth-making, prompted by the expectation of larger profits, were hitherto engaged in agriculture, because it then afforded larger profits than any other industry. In either case the motive was the same, and the directing authority—the intelligence—was the same. It was perceived that the interference of the government imposed a heavy tax on all classes of producers who had sought out and were availing themselves of, the most advantageous co-operation of the natural forces: and many were thus driven into an employment where nature's aid was so com-

the idea that the permanent cessation of imports for any cause or by any means, prevents or greatly diminishes exportation.

paratively small as to necessitate the supplemental favor of governmental protection or bounty to induce men of intelligence and capital to embark in it. But at whose cost did the government proffer this extra pay to the cloth-maker? The government itself creates no values, and can produce no wealth. In this case it simply compels all consumers to pay for imported cloth some fifty per cent. more than the natural price—for many other charges must be added to the forty per cent. duty; *or*, to pay the home manufacturer the highest price short of fifty per cent. above the natural price, that he can charge and yet exclude the foreign article.* The home manufacturer being thus strongly fortified or protected against foreign competition, naturally pays a little higher than the current rate of wages, in order to induce labor to abandon other pursuits for employment in his factory. His employés must live near the factory in which they work, and hence a village soon springs up in the neighborhood composed of people who are getting higher wages than are paid in other industries; and of merchants, artisans and others who supply the various wants of the operatives. Here, then, is an illustration of the

* Of course home competition may effect a reduction of this enhanced price after a while, but the advantage of the home manufacturer over his foreign rival remains unchanged.

beneficent effects of "protection to home industry" — a community where both capital and labor are realizing larger profits than they respectively could secure in the absence of protection. But the question constantly recurs, what are *the sources* of this exceptional prosperity? And that question admits of but one answer: the labor, the profits of all consumers who buy the protected cloth and pay for it largely in excess of the natural price.

It is very true that a small portion of customers who pay the unnatural price for cloth are enabled to share in various degrees the limited benefits of this unnatural system. Among these may be mentioned the operatives who are getting something more than ordinary wages; and the farmers and gardeners of the neighborhood who supply the villagers with agricultural products at a rate somewhat above average prices. But still the dominant fact remains, that protection has not increased the labor of the country, nor the sum of its natural forces—the indispensable factors in the production of wealth; nor has it added to its capital, nor sharpened the intellect of the people, who are always looking out for the most profitable employment for their capital and labor. It must hence follow that it has not added to the sum of wealth produced by all industries in the aggregate, and that the extraordinary prosperity of manufacturing centres so far—and *only so far*—as they are the offspring of protectionism, is wholly due to the insidious operation of the system which collects from every consumer of a protected article something in excess of its natural price, and hands it over to the favored manufacturer.

PROTECTION WORKS A DIMINUTION OF NATIONAL AND GENERAL WEALTH.

Not only does protection add nothing to the sum of wealth annually produced, but it actually and necessarily diminishes such sum—as will be made evident by a brief recapitulation: The conditions of the largest possible production consist in permitting the capital and labor of the country under the direction of the best intelligence they can bring to their aid, and entirely free from the direct or indirect intervention of the government, to form such business arrangements as will in their judgment secure the most profitable co-operation of the natural forces, and result in the largest (most valuable) product. If government interferes directly by means of bounties, or indirectly by means of protective duties, it in the former case bribes, and in the latter it drives capital and labor from associations which had been selected because in the judgment of the parties most vitally interested, such associations would prove most profitable to themselves, and would consequently add most to the wealth of the country and of the world. The difference between the value of the commodities which the given capital and labor would have produced had government not interfered, and the value of the commodities which they produced in the pursuits into which they were attracted by the largesses of the government, or driven by its veiled hostility, constitutes the measure of the loss sustained in consequence of the intermeddling of the government in business affairs.

COUNTERVAILING DUTIES.

"Perfect free trade" is admitted by Carey and other advocates of protective duties, to be the best policy for all nations; and they have often defended their own advocacy of "protection to American industry" by alleging that it is the most efficient means of constraining foreign nations to abandon import duties, of paving the way to universal free trade, and uniting all people in one common brotherhood. They admit that the levying of duties on our products by foreign nations has an injurious effect.

by lessening the consumption and consequently depressing the price of such products; they hold that being thus partially or wholly cut off, as the case may be, from the foreign market, we must create a "home market" by adopting against foreigners the same policy of exclusion as they have used against us. This argument is based on the theory that we can thus secure full indemnity for the loss occasioned by the partial or complete closing of foreign markets against our industries; and that only in this way can indemnity be secured. The question briefly stated is simply this: Suppose that all other nations imposed heavy duties on our products while we imposed none on theirs, would the imposition of countervailing duties increase the reward of labor? Keeping in view the principles laid down in the preceding pages, this question is easily and conclusively answered.

Labor is the thinking and the willing element in the process of production; matter and the forces of nature constitute the passive one. The whole domain or store-house of nature is open to labor from which it may choose its materials or invite her co-operation. It has already been shown that it is always the object of labor to make nature bear the largest possible share of the work of production. If then other nations had by the imposition of duties interfered with the natural market of some or all of our products, labor endowed with intellect would institute an examination into the effect of such legislation. It would be found that in the production of some articles nature is in all countries far more lavish of her aid than in the production of others. If the invidious legislation of foreign countries had imposed a tax on the importation of a certain article manufactured or grown in our own country, in the production of which labor had hitherto secured here its largest reward, which tax should exactly neutralize the superior degree in which nature co-operated in its production, above that of certain other articles, it would thereafter be a matter of complete indifference whether labor continued in its accustomed channel or resorted to the production of other articles assumed to be placed by the legislation referred to, in the same category as regards the profits they would yield to labor. If such legislation should impose a tax which would not fully neutralize the superior effectiveness of nature's co-operation in the case assumed, labor, guided by intellect, would still produce the same articles, because it would thus realize the largest reward. But if the tax should *more* than counterbalance the more effective co-operation of nature in producing the articles supposed, labor would then make an intelligent examination to ascertain *what articles besides* the proscribed ones nature would assist most in producing. And having found the articles in the production of which, under all the circumstances, nature would be most liberal in her favors, and thus secure to human industry the largest net reward, labor would enter into this new field; and thus free trade would leave the matter so far as we are concerned, conscious that the legislation of other nations affected injuriously the industry of our people; but that all attempts to compensate ourselves for these injuries by means of "protective" duties levied on goods consumed by ourselves, would simply aggravate the evils for which they are urged as a remedy.

TRANSPORTATION CONSIDERED IN ITS ECONOMICAL ASPECTS.

" Protection," says H. C. Carey, " seeks to cause the loom and the anvil to take their natural places by the side of the food and the cotton." *

" One of the chief waste-gates of human effort is that afforded by the consumption of time and energies in the transportation across oceans and continents of staples or fabrics which might as easily—

* Carey's " Harmony of Interests," p. 72.

that is with little or no more labor—have been produced in the region where they are required and consumed."

"I want to save the millions on millions thus annually expended—I believe uselessly, wastefully expended. I want to divide them between the grower and the consumer of Tea, or to secure them to him where the same person shall be both grower and consumer. I believe that to pursue this policy is to increase the reward of labor generally, and especially of American labor." *

There is a plausibility in this method of presenting a great economical question which captivates and misleads many minds; but it includes no argument whatever, and warrants no conclusion. Carey neither in the short extract quoted, nor elsewhere in all his voluminous works, proves to the logical mind, that the legislative power of a great nation must be put in requisition in order to "cause" or to enable "the loom and the anvil," or any other machines, elements or factors of production "to take their natural places." The authority of a powerful government wielded by men not versed in economical science, is not unfrequently exerted "to cause the loom and the anvil to take *un*natural places;" but left to herself, Nature will prove her own best administrator.

* Greeley's "Political Economy—Art, Commerce and Exchanges."

The proposition that intelligent men, seeking the best return for their capital and labor, will not put "the loom and the anvil"—a phrase designed to include productive machinery generally—in their "natural places," *i. e.*, where such machinery will produce the largest net values, would seem to be too absurd to merit serious consideration. Turning to Greeley's "argument," it will be observed that it is based entirely on his "belief" that "millions on millions are wastefully expended in transportation across oceans and continents," which he benevolently " wants to save!" But the real questions are, will "the loom and the anvil take their natural places" without governmental coercion; and are the millions paid for transporting the products of a people intelligently engaged in industries which in their judgment are the most profitable, and in the selection of which the government has not undertaken to exercise the least influence—are the millions so paid " uselessly, wastefully expended?"

Now grant that a "staple," say iron for instance, has been transported across the ocean for use in a "region" where coal and iron ore are abundant, and that " with little or no more labor" than was expended in making it abroad, it " might have been produced in the region where it was required and consumed;" it does not hence necessarily follow that the money paid for transporting it was "uselessly, wastefully expended," as may be easily shown. For, suppose a given quantity of labor would produce a cargo, say one thousand tons, of iron abroad, and that the same quantity of labor devoted to making iron in Pennsylvania would produce one thousand tons of iron; but that the same quantity of labor devoted to agriculture would produce grain enough to pay for twelve hundred tons of foreign iron delivered in Pennsylvania. In such a case it is perfectly clear there would be no loss in consequence of importing iron instead of "producing it in the region where it is required." Labor recognizing a demand for iron, and being free to avail itself of the natural forces under such conditions as it deemed most advantageous, concluded as the result of intelligent calculation, that it could procure the iron by raising grain and exchanging it for a foreign article, at a less cost in labor or money than a like article would cost if made at home. Under such circumstances the leading industry of the "region" in question, would be agriculture; simply because in that industry given labor would produce greater net values than it could in making iron. Should the time ever come—as in fact it has already come in this country—when, for any reason or combination of reasons, the iron and coal mines which had hitherto remained untouched, could be worked at a profit and without burdening other industries, *then* a portion of the labor and capital of the country directed by the same intelligence, and prompted by the same motive that had hitherto prevented the building of furnaces and rolling-mills, would embark in the iron manufacture. But that time cannot be hastened by legislative action; nor is it in the slightest degree probable, that a few politicians and statesmen in Parliament or "Congress assembled," will be able to discern the fact that it *has* arrived, at an earlier day or with more unerring certainty than the prudent and sagacious employer of labor, who, while he profits by his own far-sightedness and enterprise, must also pay the penalty of his own mistakes.

A very simple and candid examination of the respective cases, shows clearly that the money paid for transporting iron to Pennsylvania was not "uselessly, wastefully expended," and that the labor devoted to grain-growing in Iowa as the cheapest mode of securing a supply of clothing was not misdirected. But the full amount of benefit accruing to the people and to the country from the free exchange policy which these two cases are intended to illustrate, has not yet appeared. It has simply been shown that the principals in the two transactions acted wisely. Their object in either case was to get the largest quantity possible of a certain commodity, for a given quantity of labor. The difference between the quantity of the respective commodities which given labor could secure by means of exchange, and the quantity which it could produce at home, would indicate with tolerable accuracy the advantage which, in these operations, the free-trade policy possesses over its rival. Its supplemental benefits remain to be considered.

The Iowa case is best suited to this purpose, since it is already familiar to the reader, it is presented as a typical case and it involves long lines of transportation and heavy charges for commissions and freights in the exchange of "the staples and fabrics" which it includes. These charges are set forth by the protectionists as money "uselessly, wastefully expended," whereas an intelligent and careful examination of the processes and incidents of commerce will show that no part of this money is uselessly or wastefully expended; but that on the contrary a goodly portion of it accrues as profits to capital and labor, which but for the exchange of "staples and fabrics" produced in regions far apart, would never be realized at all.

The exchange of Iowa wheat for a cargo of English cloths, whether effected directly between parties producing and owning the respective commodities, or indirectly through the agency of professional importers, necessarily implies that the purchasers in either case have paid all charges incident to transporting the staples or fabrics across the ocean and the continent, and that they regard the transaction as a profitable one to themselves. These charges go to pay the wages of the railway engine-driver, firemen, conductors, brakemen, freight agents and other employés; also to pay the wages of the captains, subordinate officers, sailors, and others employed on the ships which carry these staples and fabrics across the ocean; also to pay the profits on the capital invested in the railways, ships and other machinery used in this long line of transportation; and yet further, to pay bankers and others such commissions as are incident to international trade. Every one of the parties who has contributed a portion of his labor or capital to facilitate the exchange of commodities produced thousands of miles apart, has done so because in his opinion he could thus make a more profitable use of his labor or capital than he could in any other way. So that not only have the principals in the transaction made a more profitable use of their time and money than they could make in any other; but everybody who has participated in it directly or indirectly, has done the same thing. For all these benefits, liberally distributed along a line thousands of miles in length, nature should be credited; since on the hypothesis nature offers to man such advantageous terms of co-operation for the production of grain in Iowa, and for the manufacture of cloth in England, that these two commodities can be produced in regions so far apart and then exchanged one for the other, not only without loss, but with a profit to the producers and to all engaged in exchanging them, larger than they respectively could realize in other investments or pursuits. If it be objected that the hypothesis is not in harmony with nature or facts, the only answer that is necessary is simply this: the moment that it ceases to be true, that the conditions it embodies are so changed that the profits which enter into it can no longer be realized, that moment the exchange of Iowa grain for English cloths will cease, even though the government should not interfere to stop it by means of protective duties. Moreover, the hypothesis is borrowed from a protectionist, Greeley, who used it to convey to his readers a striking idea of the absurdity and wastefulness of raising grain in the west, transporting it " across oceans and continents," buying with the proceeds and transporting all the way back to the west, English fabrics " which might as easily, that is, with little or no more labor, have been produced in the region where they are required and consumed." It has been used here to show that so long as a commerce of the kind described is carried on, the very fact of its existence is conclusive proof that it is neither absurd nor profitless, and that when it ceases to be profitable to those engaged in it, they will at once abandon it in obedience to the dictates of self-interest, and the obnoxious commerce will then be carried on no more.

It may be observed here briefly, that the same principles which enter into and control the case above considered, enter into and control all kinds of enterprises and industries to which men devote their labor, their capital and their skill. All writers on political economy admit that all men are controlled by their own opinion as to what will pay them best, when seeking employment for themselves or their capital. The parties to the international commerce referred to above were true to that rule of action. They continued to exchange their respective products regardless of distance and expense, so long as the result was a satisfactory net profit to each; and when they could no longer realize a satisfactory profit from that kind of business, they left it and engaged in another.

THE "NATURAL PLACES" FOR MANUFACTURING MACHINERY.

What perplexes the protectionists and confuses their judgment, is the fact that while Iowa, for instance, contains all the elements required for making cloth—such as a soil and climate adapted to wool-growing, water-power, intelligent labor, etc.—yet, in the absence of governmental interference cloth can be obtained at less cost by raising grain and exchanging it for cloth made in England. They insist that inasmuch as Iowa indisputably comprises all the conditions required for making cloth, therefore the "natural place" for the woollen factory must necessarily be Iowa; and that if man will persist in agricultural and other industries, but will not voluntarily use his money to put "the loom and the anvil in their natural places," he should be constrained to do so by appropriate legislation.

Now, grant that Iowa does offer all the conditions necessary for simply *making* cloth, it does not necessarily follow that Iowa is the "natural place" for the woollen mill. To make it such "place" one more condition, and that an indispensable one, is required: that cloth can be *produced* in Iowa at less cost than it can be *procured* there in exchange for other products of the same region. When these several conditions become facts, then, but not until then, will Iowa really be " the natural place " for the manufacture of woollens.

The advocates of protective duties, when urging the government to pass such or such laws in order "to cause the loom and the anvil to take their natural places by the side of the food and the cotton," strangely forget or ignore the fact that the very coercive intervention they invoke necessarily implies that the "places" in question are *not* "natural" to the symbolized industries. What is really "natural" in regard to the various industries, will certainly occur if no obstacle is interposed. Nothing, surely, can be more natural than the unobstructed operation of the natural laws. The conduct of man as a producer, as an element in political economy, is as absolutely controlled by natural laws as the motion of the heavenly bodies. But the protectionists seem to omit the element that calculates and wills, when they undertake to solve the problem: "What is natural in respect to placing the loom and anvil?" Here is cotton and here is food; here then is the natural place for the loom. There is iron ore and there is coal; there then is the natural place for the anvil. Thus they reason. But they have left out an element, whose absence vitiates all their arguments and conclusions.

Suppose this method be applied to some other industries. Of thousands of localities in the United States it may be truly said: here is a sand bank and here is a clay bed close by; this then is the natural place for a brick kiln. Let the government foster the brick manufacture until more of these natural places are occupied. A little way inland all along our coast is excellent ship timber, which is easily brought down to the sea. Let the government interpose to protect this natural national industry. Finally, here, everywhere you tread the surface of "mother earth," who invites your co-operation in the production of food and raiment for all her children. Is not agriculture then the most "natural" of all industries? If man is so purblind as not to see nature beckoning him to cultivate the soil in preference to seeking for treasure in the bowels of the earth or in commerce over tempestuous seas, what can be more fit for government to do, than by the imposition of adequate penalties to compel its subjects to abandon their unnatural industries for the natural, and the perilous for the safe?

This line of remark or "argument" might be pursued to any extent; and it could hardly fail to convince the candid and intelligent that the way to secure the largest and most profitable production, is to leave man to make such arrangements for the employment of his capital and labor as he may judge most advantageous, entirely free from governmental dictation or interference.

THE CONVERSION OF IDLERS INTO PRODUCERS.

Greeley considers "the chief end of a true political economy to be the conversion of idlers and useless exchangers into habitual, effective producers of wealth." Protection, he holds, naturally effects this conversion.

It has already been demonstrated that "exchangers" are not a "useless" part of the people. As to the "conversion of idlers," it may well be asked how, at whose expense, and for whose benefit it may be effected? It has been shown, that the only way protection can lead to a "diversity of pursuits" is by driving labor from the more profitable associations with nature to the less profitable. The sum of labor's earnings would thus be necessarily less, and it would be less equitably distributed, than it would be under a policy of non-interference on the part of the government. Hence, if protection benefits those who would otherwise be "idlers," it must do so at the expense of a better class—and at a cost to them in excess of the benefits conferred on the less worthy.

PROTECTIONISM AND COMMERCE.

It has been very aptly said that error is always forced into inconsistencies in order to invest its arguments and conclusions with any degree of plausibility. This is well illustrated in the writings of Carey and other protectionists. Their most specious argument, and the one most likely to take with the multitude, is, that commerce necessarily involves immense waste, which protection prevents for the benefit of the producer and consumer—in short, for the benefit of all mankind. The "millions on millions paid for transportation across oceans and continents," they allege are "uselessly, wastefully expended," as has already been noted. All these millions it is the appointed mission of their policy to save and add to the profits of labor and capital. All the machinery of exchange, such as railways, wagons, ships, etc., according to their theory, are used and worn out in the unproductive work of exchanging commodities, which under the wiser system of protection, might and would be produced in the same region. Carey is so comprehensive and circumstantial in his inventory of the savings of his favorite policy as to include the manure of draught animals dropped on the road while employed in the "useless and wasteful" business of drawing back and forth the products of contiguous neighborhoods! This class of arguments goes to the absolute annihilation of commerce and exchange, not only between nations, but also between different portions of the same country. For as Carey would proscribe the "internal commerce" carried on by means of the wagon and the ox-cart, so Greeley has recorded his opinion that Iowa would be greatly benefited by an interstate protective tariff which should exclude the fabrics of the Eastern States and "cause the loom to take its natural place" by the side of the grain-fields of that agricultural State. "Protection," says he in another place,* "dispenses with long and perilous voyages and the costly movement of bulky raw materials across oceans and continents to recompense and subsist artisans engaged in the production of metals, wares and fabrics for the use of the producers of these raw materials, securing a larger recompense, a more generous subsistence, to either class by relieving them of the useless expense of

* Greeley's "Political Economy," p. 283.

maintaining the army of speculators, forwarders, boatmen, shippers, railway operators, etc., etc., formerly interposed between them, and bringing them into direct and economic relationship as members of the same community."

To the same effect, H. C. Carey affirms "if they (the United States) determine that they will eat their own food and work up their own cotton, and smelt their own iron ore, the downfall of the system of ships, commerce and colonies, is as certain to take place as it is now certain that the navigation and corn laws have been repealed." *

It is perfectly clear that such language as is quoted above, from eminent protectionist authorities, contemplates the utter extinction of all commerce and all trade, excepting at most, such local traffic as may be carried on between inhabitants of the same little neighborhood or precinct.

But while uttering these maledictions against commerce, and especially against foreign commerce, and foretelling its "downfall" as one of the "certain" consequences of an efficient protective system, they did not seem to give full credence to their own arguments and prophecies. Indeed, when they come to address the commercial classes—whose combined action might be dangerous to a high tariff policy—

* "Present, Past and Future," p. 455.

they agree, in apparent good faith, that the most effectual way to stimulate an external foreign commerce is to impose a heavy penalty on all who engage in it, in the form of an enormous tax or protective duty on almost every foreign article they offer to sell us, and to levy such tax or duty with the avowed purpose of diminishing importations! Carey says: "Commerce had grown with protection." "Commerce has fallen with the diminution of protection." "The interests of commerce are therefore in perfect harmony with those of manufactures." "Commerce withers under free trade." "The commerce of India diminishes with every approach to what is called free trade." "Abolish protection and commerce will diminish." "I think I see why it is that shipping grows with protection." *

Greeley, too, enters into an elaborate argument to establish the same proposition: In 1824, Daniel Webster, then a free trader, opposed protection as a policy hostile to navigation and foreign commerce. But the tariff act which he opposed passed in spite of his efforts. Comparing official returns referring to the four years next preceding, with those of four years next succeeding the passage of that act, Greeley finds that American tonnage had increased over twenty per cent.; the number of ships built in

---

* "Harmony of Interests," pp. 72, 73, 90.

in the latter four years was more than fifty per cent. greater than that built in the former four years; and the receipts from duties on imports during the latter period showed an advance over the former of about thirty-three per cent. Greeley's purpose in presenting these statistics is of course to prove that the growth of commerce and ship-building was attributable to the levying of higher import duties. But statistical arguments in such cases possess little or no value; since it can neither be shown that the results under consideration were not mainly or wholly due to some other than the cause assigned, nor that the growth in ship-building and commerce would not have been greater had there been no increase in the duties on imports.

Such strange "reasoning" might well be dismissed without further comment. Yet it may, perhaps, be worth while to call attention to the fact that the two most eminent and influential protectionist writers our country has produced, have deliberately affirmed, in published volumes, that efficient "protection to home industry" would certainly effect "the downfall of ships, commerce and colonies," would extirpate "the army of forwarders, boatmen, shippers, railway operators, etc.," and would "save millions on millions uselessly, wastefully expended annually" in freights; and on the other hand, they have affirmed as positively that "protection to home industry" promotes the growth of commerce, adds to the number of American ships, and imparts a wholesome activity to trade generally. Human ingenuity is inadequate to the reconciliation of such antagonistic arguments and pretensions. Had they limited their efforts to showing the superior advantages of internal over foreign commerce, they might at least have avoided these glaring inconsistencies.

ADAM SMITH AND SAY ON INTERNAL AND FOREIGN TRADE.

Adam Smith, often styled the father of free trade, has laid down one proposition, which, were it true, would not only make foreign commerce a losing business, but would render it impossible. Jean Baptiste Say has indorsed Smith's position; and the authority of both is invoked by Carey's disciple, E. Peshine Smith, in support of protectionism. Adam Smith held that even "though the returns of the foreign trade of consumption should be as quick as those of the home trade, it will give but one-half of the encouragement to the industry or productive labor of the country.*

And Say says: "The internal commerce of a

* "Wealth of Nations," Book II., chap. v.

country * * * * sets in motion a double production, and the profits of it are not participated with foreigners."*

No argument can be necessary to convince any sane man that if, as a rule, foreign trade would pay only one-half the profits of home trade, foreign trade would immediately and entirely cease. But everybody not possessed with a "dominant idea" of contrary tenor, must readily see that these great authorities have made a mistake.

Expected profits supply the natural stimulus or " encouragement to the industry or productive labor of the country." The sending of Scotch manufactures to London, and bringing back in exchange the products of English industry, Smith regards as highly advantageous, because the profits realized by the producers and carriers of both the Scotch and English commodities accrue to British subjects, and are retained in the country. The profits actually secured by all parties to the transaction, constitute the measure of the " encouragement" it has afforded to " the industry of the country." Now suppose, as Smith does, that one of these parties sends his goods to Portugal and brings back Portuguese goods, the question arises, *why* does he do so ; and the only answer the case admits of is, because he makes more

* Say's " Political Economy," Book I., chap. ix.

profit than he was making by sending his goods to the London market. Suppose the other party sends his goods to France and takes his pay in French goods, the same explanation applies to his case : he thus makes more profit than he was making by sending his goods to Scotland. The net result of these transactions with foreigners, is a larger sum of profits than the parties realized when trading with each other. These profits have all been secured and they form, after the close of the transactions, a part of the capital of the country ; and by the amount which such profits exceed the profits which would have been realized in the home trade, the foreign has surpassed the home trade in affording " encouragement to the industry of the country."

But assuming for a moment that Smith's argument is sound, let its application be reversed : here are two capitals (one Portuguese, the other French) devoted to making goods for the British market. Each makes but one-half the profit it would make were its products exchanged for other products of its own country. Who, in these several cases, gets the half of the profits which the exporting country loses? Does the "party of the other part?"—then the loss and the gain are mutual, and they balance each other. Does nobody get them; and is the loss compensated by no corresponding gain? Then it must fall on some individual parties who will need no other incentive to make them withdraw from so ruinous a trade.

Let us look at the matter under slightly altered conditions: Suppose Scotland and England were separate sovereignties, as they were before the union; in that case, according to Adam Smith's theory, the trade between London and Edinburgh would have been comparatively damaging to both parties instead of being advantageous to both, as he represents it. Both parties being regarded as Britons, trade between them is held to be beneficial to both, and to their country; but one being regarded as a Scotchman and the other an Englishman, trade between them, if not positively damaging, is held to be but one-half as beneficial as if both owed political allegiance to the same Sovereign! The protectionists of our country still cling most tenaciously to the same fallacy. They cannot disabuse their minds of the delusion that commerce—the mere exchange of equivalent values, as they admit it to be—with a fellow-citizen or subject, is profitable; whereas the same exchange with a foreigner would be less profitable, if not a losing operation. Thus Carey says: "We are all free-trade men. We all feel the benefits resulting from the existence of that freedom in the intercourse between the various States of the Union, and we all know that great advantage must result from the establishment of similar freedom among the various nations of the world whenever it shall become possible." *

On another occasion, he reiterates these views still more emphatically: " The annexation of the land and the people of Canada and the other British possessions would enlarge the domain of perfect free trade. So would that of Cuba, Mexico, Ireland, and even England; and the free trade thus established would be beneficial to all, the annexers and the annexed." †

The delusion already noted will be rendered the more striking by placing in juxtaposition with the above, language uttered by the same author almost in the same breath. The following is taken from the third page preceding the extract quoted: " The object of the now dominant class in England is that of bringing about free trade with the world. Such a measure adopted by this country would close every furnace and rolling-mill, and every cotton and woollen factory in the country, and would diminish the value of both labor and land, by compelling the producer of food to seek a market in England." ‡

* Letter to R. J. Walker, p. 4.
† Carey's " Harmony of Interests," p. 135.   ‡ Id. p. 132.

That is, free trade "established" by commercial treaty between England and the United States would prove utterly ruinous to all our great interests—both manufacturing and agricultural. But free trade "established" by a treaty of annexation, "would be beneficial to all, the annexers and the annexed!"

It seems hardly possible that doctrines so conflicting, not to say so absurd, can be entertained by men of ordinary intelligence. Yet just such doctrines are, and long have been, theoretically asserted and resolutely enforced by the government of this country—as a single illustration will show: A railway three hundred yards in length, spanning Niagara river, connects two active little villages, one British, the other American; and at a short distance behind these villages on either side, are situated populous and wealthy cities, inhabited by people whose language, origin, modes of life, religious faiths, tastes and industries are substantially alike, and to whom this suspended railway affords the most direct and natural means of inter-communication. At the American end of this railway bridge, a number of government officials are always stationed to prevent free trade with the people of the other side, and save all our manufacturing and agricultural industries from utter ruin—which the mere exchange of equivalent values across this bridge would certainly occasion! But from the same point on the American side, a series of railways three thousand miles in length extend to the Pacific coast. California has been "annexed;" "free trade *thus* established" is "beneficial to all;" and as a consequence of the prevalence of the doctrines under consideration, the trade over the three thousand miles of railway is left open and free to all, while trade over the three hundred yards of railway is embarrassed and obstructed by the government, lest it should ruin the people!"*

COMMERCE.

Putting aside or omitting from the discussion mere local traffic in commodities produced in the same neighborhood, the term Commerce will be considered here very briefly as applying to the exchange of the products of different countries or of distant sections of the same country.

As thus defined, commerce may be divided into

---

*The reciprocity treaty, now awaiting action by the two governments, if agreed to, would somewhat change the state of things now existing. But the doctrines commented on above, would continue to be asserted and enforced in respect to all our foreign commerce, excepting only so much as would be affected by that treaty.

two kinds. 1st. That which brings to the consumer commodities which under ordinary conditions cannot be produced in his section of country, such as tea, coffee, and the tropical fruits for example, with reference to the northern portions of Europe and America; and 2d, that which brings to the consumer commodities which under ordinary conditions are produced there, but not in quantities sufficient to supply the demand. This latter kind only has any special relevancy to my present purpose. The two high protectionist authorities already quoted, it will be remembered, look upon "exchangers" and "transporters" as men who must "be supported out of the labor of the farmers and planters." * A more rational view would regard them as co-producers with the farmers and planters. Suppose, for illustration, New England requires a larger quantity of the coarser grains than that section of country ordinarily produces. Her intelligent people are aware that they can produce a full supply from their own soil; but in order to do so they would be obliged to plant so large a portion of the cultivable land that there would be too little left to supply hay and pasture, etc., etc., which their necessities would require. In any event there would be a deficit in one or more agricultural products. Commerce—" the transporters, con-

* Carey's "Harmony of Interests," p. 83.

verters and exchangers"—now steps in, in the character of a producer. Nature offers so much more favorable terms of co-operation for the production of the required cereals in Michigan, Illinois and Iowa than she does in New England, that Commerce sets her laborers at work in the west to raise the grain; and then sets her "transporters, converters and exchangers" at work to gather it up and deliver it in quantities to suit purchasers in the Eastern States. Commerce in this case, in so far as results are concerned, performs all the functions of producer, and successfully competes with all other producers in the same industry. What was required was a larger supply of given cereals in New England; and Commerce, with characteristic sagacity and enterprise, instead of delving away at her rugged soil to get it, grew it on more fertile soils far away, but "produced" it when and where wanted, and at less cost than it could be grown at or nearer home. If California and Great Britain be substituted for our Eastern and Western States, no essential feature of the case will require modification. Hundreds of ship loads of wheat are annually transported from the first to the last named country—a distance almost equal to the circumference of the globe. Britain is itself one of the great wheat producing countries of the world. Yet her industries sustain so large a population that her own product of breadstuffs is far short of their wants. According to the theories of the protectionist authorities, so often quoted in the preceding pages—that distances between producer and consumer should be shortened as much as possible, and by means of governmental interference if other means prove unavailing; and that commerce should generally follow the "lines of longitude" rather than those of latitude, so as to effect an exchange of the products of different "zones:"—according to these theories Britain should perhaps eke out her supply of bread-stuffs with the rice of warmer climates, instead of "wasting" so much money and labor in transporting from the other side of the globe, a supply of wheat which "might be" produced at home! But these theories are the result of inattention to, or partial observation of, facts—which is quite usual with their authors. A producer of any one of the great staples which are consumed by civilized man everywhere, knows perfectly well that his fellow-men who live in a "zone" where his own product cannot be successfully cultivated, must follow "the lines of longitude" to the "zone" where it is successfully cultivated in order to procure it. But the line of longitude is only one of many indications where to look for a purchaser of a given product; and it is by no means one of the safest indications. What the producer wants is a purchaser; and what the consumer wants is a producer, or an intermediary who can supply the given commodity at the lowest attainable price. Whether these parties find each other by following longitudinal or latitudinal or diagonal lines, is to them a matter of perfect indifference. Trusting to such theories as Greeley propounds, one would expect to find the surplus products of Northern Europe mostly exchanged for the surplus products of equatorial Africa, instead of being transported along isothermal lines and exchanged for products of the same "zone" as that in which they were produced. If "let alone," the producer and the consumer, inspired by their own self-interest and guided by their own intelligence and sagacity, will find each other and effect their exchanges by availing themselves of the least expensive routes and instrumentalities. And having done that, they will have done what is best, not only for their own interests, but also what is best for the interests of all others who finally consume any portion of the commodities thus produced and exchanged.

For the purposes of this work, the above is a sufficiently full and accurate epitome of all the facts and forces which give rise to the kind of exchanges under consideration—the position, relation and motives of those who aid in effecting them, having been already treated of in a preceding chapter.

SUNDRY OTHER PROTECTIONIST ARGUMENTS AND POSITIONS, BRIEFLY NOTICED.

As my principal object in this work is to prove that protection cannot possibly cause an increase in the production of values because it possesses no means of adding to the quantity or the activity or the efficiency of the necessary forces or factors of production, I might well have omitted to notice the arguments, assumptions and sophistries, by means of . which its advocates have long led popular opinion astray. Yet it seemed to me not inappropriate—as it certainly does not conflict with my main object— to point out as briefly as may be, some of the fallacies, inconsistencies and absurdities in which the protectionist school are accustomed to indulge. Some of these have already been disposed of; a few others only will receive attention here.

THE TIME PLEA.

From the beginning of our high tariff legislation to the present day, its supporters have been in the habit of meeting objections to so partial a system, by representing it as only a temporary expedient, to be maintained until our people should be schooled to the favored industries and the capital therein invested should become fairly remunerative; and then to be discarded for free trade, which they, it is believed without exception, profess to regard as the fairest and best system, and for the permanent establishment of which protection is designed to prepare the way. But the time for discarding the temporary and probational, and adopting the ultimate and true system, seems destined to be forever postponed. Thus so long ago as 1833, Henry Clay, " the father of the American system," in a speech advocating protection, delivered in the Senate of the United States, said: "Now give us *time;* cease all fluctuations and agitations for nine years, and the manufacturers in every branch will sustain themselves against foreign competition." *

If any man was ever authorized to speak for or in behalf of the protectionists of this country, nobody will dispute that Henry Clay was that man. Thirty-six years later,—after four times the period of nine years had elapsed—Horace Greeley wrote his " Political coEnomy," which he dedicated " to the memory of Henry Clay, * * the man who most effectually

* " Clay's Speeches," Vol. II. p. 147.

commended the policy of protection to the understandings and hearts of the masses of his countrymen." In this work the author, speaking of the duty on pig iron, says, " that duty is exactly nine dollars per ton, which is one dollar less than it was by the Calhoun-Lowndes tariff of 1816—is the lowest specific duty ever imposed on pig iron in any tariff from 1815 to 1861 inclusive; I believe it is doing good—nay,* *I know* it. * * Let it be settled

---

* The italics are Greeley's. He, like most other protectionists, has a chronic habit of making his own knowledge, real or assumed, and even his belief, answer the purpose of argument. "I *know* it," proceeding fron Horace Greeley, was quite sufficient to secure the acceptance of his high tariff theories by tens of thousands of his readers—and he "*knew* it!" So well did he "know it" that he relied on the influence of his own convictions and unsupported assertions in enforcing his protectionist dogmas, far more than upon reason. In one of his short chapters the pronoun "I" occurs no less than thirty-four times. The same "method" is very extensively patronized by Carey in his economical writings. Indeed this, or some similar method, becomes a sort of necessity, when the object of the writer is to convince his readers of the truth of a proposition or theory which will not stand the test of sound methods of reasoning.

The partisans of protectionism also prop up their system by quotations from the "revolutionary fathers" and others of cherished memory, but who are no more entitled to be quoted as authority in political economy, than in medicine or theology. Thus Dr. Franklin, perhaps more frequently cited than any of his contemporaries in scientific discussions, at one time advocated an irredeemable paper money "secured" by real-estate mortgages, and Edmund Burke upheld the same "system" so modified as to substitute debased coin for paper. [Bancroft's Hist. United States, Vol. III. pp. 388–90.] Henry Clay quoted Count Nesselrode to prove that manufactures, agriculture and commerce, would *all* be ruined by free trade—unless all nations should adopt it. [Clay's Speeches, pp.

and understood that the duty will be maintained, and we shall have a thousand more furnaces in operation within the next two years." *

Precisely why the maintenance of "the lowest specific duty ever imposed on pig iron, in any tariff from 1815 to 1861, inclusive," would set "one thousand more furnaces in operation within the next two years" succeeding 1869, the author fails to explain. On a previous occasion he had remarked that protection is "not a philosophy;" and probably no attentive reader of even the few extracts from the writings of protectionists, which have been quoted in the preceding pages, will feel disposed to controvert that position. It is worthy of mention, in this connection, that from and including 1815 to the present time, pig iron has enjoyed just sixty years of protection against the competition of foreign iron makers. Yet the iron interest in this country still demands protection as sturdily as it did sixty years ago. The plea for a little more time would seem to be no longer admissible.

255–6.] And while Clay depended on the opinion of the first Napoleon, Count Nesselrode and others of high position and rank, to sustain his views on economical questions, he classed political economists with "novelists and metaphysicians!" [Ib. p. 156.]

* Greeley's "Political Economy," pp. 217, 18.

PROTECTION AGAINST CHEAP FOREIGN LABOR.

The protectionists for more than half a century have labored zealously to impress the public mind with the idea that but for a protective tariff, the products of the cheap (often styled the *pauper*) labor of Europe would be sent hither and sold at such low prices as to ruin the prosperity of the whole country. Our manufacturing industry would "be overwhelmed by foreign competition," says Greeley; and according to the same authority "the bulk and weight of most agricultural staples forbid their transportation to remote markets, *except at ruinous cost.*" Hence the necessary conclusion, that in the absence of protection, we could not *manufacture* commodities at home because of the presence of like foreign commodities offered to us at less cost than we could produce them; and we could not *buy* the foreign commodities because our products would be agricultural staples, which could not be transported to remote markets and sold, "except at ruinous cost!" Thus easily is protection shown to be a most beneficent system, which is scarcely possible to extol too highly!

But the fallacy of this mode of "reasoning" consists in asserting as true of "the national industry,"—that is, of all industries in the aggregate,—what is or may be true of certain limited and special industries. The manufacturer of a given highly protected commodity might be ruined by the repeal of the duty which protects him from foreign competition and enables him to get from fifteen to forty per cent. more for his products than similar foreign products would otherwise be sold for; but it is a manifest absurdity to assume that the repeal of that duty would ruin both the manufacturer, who is profiting so largely by it, and the consumers of his products, who are losing more or less largely because it is not repealed.

But again; the partisans of the high tariff policy allege, that though cheaper in " money price," the foreign products would really be dearer than the domestic ones, because of the " ruinous cost " on agricultural staples," the sale of which, in " remote markets," would be necessary in order to get money with which to buy the foreign manufactures. The question at once arises, on whom would this " ruinous cost " fall? If on the producer of the heavy and bulky " agricultural staples," he would need no admonition from legislator or author that he must apply his capital and labor to other industries. The same remark is applicable to the "transporters and exchangers," and to all other parties interested in that particular industry. Moreover all men of intelligence, to whatever school of political economy they may belong, know well that the sales and purchases, the production and consumption (using the terms in the larger sense), of men and nations, necessarily balance each other. Thus H. C. Carey, who has written volumes to convince his countrymen that the exercise of the natural rights of man to engage in such lawful industry as he may find most profitable, and to sell or exchange the products of his industry in the markets of the world if left unfettered by legislative intervention, would work the impoverishment of his country and the subversion of all its important industries: even he is constrained to say, "it is essential that it be recollected, *every man is a consumer to the whole extent of his production, whatever that may be.*"*

"The extent of his production," therefore, constitutes the measure of his ability to consume. Then if he produced nothing, he could ruin neither the country nor himself by buying the cheap products of the "pauper labor" of foreign lands, since he would have nothing to buy them with. But if he did produce values in any form more or less abundantly, the exchange of these for equivalent values in other

* Carey's "Harmony of Interests," p. 115. The italics are his.

forms; that is, the exchange of commodities which he produced for commodities of equal value produced by others, whether in our own or in foreign lands, could neither impoverish him nor derange the industries of the country. It is indisputable that the sum of the products of individuals constitutes the aggregate of national production; and that the sum of the wealth of its citizens constitutes the wealth of the nation. The object of each producer is to get the largest, that is, the most valuable return for the labor, the capital and the skill which he uses or employs in the work of production. If he cannot with safety to his own and the public interests, be allowed to choose what industries to embark in, how is it possible that on placing him in the legislative halls, or on his becoming an editor or an author, he should suddenly become competent to decide what industries and occupations his fellow-citizens must follow in order to secure the largest profits, and what ones they must eschew in order to avert national ruin?

Let us look at this bugbear of pauper labor and cheap products in another aspect. The protectionist position, briefly stated, is simply this: Wages are so low and capital so abundant and cheap in Europe, that in the absence of protection the products of her factories and work-shops would be offered in our markets at such low prices as to render competition impossible, and our home industries would be paralyzed and overthrown. American labor and capital must therefore be protected from the free competition of foreign manufacturers, by means of a tax on imports, in order to preserve our home industries from absolute and certain ruin. Hence the watchwords, "protection to home industry," and "protection to home labor."

But our "home industries" are not a unit; nor are their interests or the interests of all "home labor" homogeneous and identical. The demand for "protection to American manufactures," for instance, is made in the interest of the *producer*, NOT of the *consumer* of the commodity seeking protection from foreign competition. While, however, they desire such protection for commodities of their own production, they assume to demand it in the name and behalf of the interests of American industry and home labor!

No man was ever ruined pecuniarily because he paid so little for the commodities he and his family consumed; or in other words, because he received too much of the produce of others' labor in return for a given quantity of his own. Yet the pecuniary object of protection is to raise the price to consumers of all the articles to which it applies; since if it did not raise the price, the producer would derive no benefit from it.

The purpose of all labor and every industry, is to produce or procure commodities to supply the wants of man. Now, suppose foreigners, by some mysterious process, could produce and deliver on our shores, without cost to themselves, all the foreign products we have been accustomed to get by the exchange of the proceeds of our own industries, and that they should offer to do so without cost to us—would the acceptance of their offer prove destructive to the interests of American industry and home labor, using these terms in a comprehensive and the only proper sense? Will protectionists seriously affirm that the interests of home industry and labor would be benefited by declining a proffered gift of all such products? Can they possibly conceive how the American people in the aggregate could profit more by giving the proceeds of, say two hundred million days' labor, in exchange for such products than they would by accepting them as a free gift?

But if their imagination is adequate to such a conception, are they capable of going further and conceiving how the acceptance of such gifts would prove damaging to those of our people who consume the products it comprises, and who are not interested in the manufacture of similar products? If not, as they are certainly not capable of conceiving anything of the kind, they will at least be forced to the conclusion that American interests are not all homogeneous and identical; and that when they propose to protect home industries and home labor by means of a tax on imports, their proposition necessarily implies the promotion of certain classes of interests at the expense of certain other classes of interests.

It is safe to assume that the most ardent protectionist could not conjure up reasons satisfactory to himself, nor convincing to the simplest understanding among the mass of consumers, to justify the refusal of a proffered gift of all foreign products which we have been accustomed to pay for with the proceeds of our own industries and labor; and if they could not justify a declension of the hypothetical gift, they cannot *logically* justify a refusal to *purchase* such products, if offered to us, at fifty per cent. or other large discount, in lieu of the prices we had hitherto paid. For, consider the matter in an economic sense, there is no difference in principle between declining the gift of a commodity one requires to satisfy his wants, and declining to buy it at a reduction of twenty or fifty per cent. below the usual price, simply *because* the price is too low. If the acceptance of the commodity as a gift would be advantageous, the purchase of the same commodity at much less than its usual cost would be advantageous, though not as advantageous as if it were a gift. And if the purchase at such low price would prove disastrous to American labor and American industries, the gift would necessarily prove far more disastrous to American labor and American industries.

" Augustus was sensible that mankind is governed by names."* He accordingly imposed tyranny in the name of liberty. Parties in-interested in a high tariff policy, "sensible" like Augustus, manage to impose crushing and oppressive taxes on the great mass of their countrymen in the name of "protection." The victims of the imposture not only submit to it, but support and applaud those who profit by it, as the Romans did before them. How absolute their delusion becomes, may perhaps be made more apparent by a simple illustration : There is scarcely a person in the United States of any class or condition, who does not every year consume more or less of foreign made fabrics of wool and cotton. Let us consider only the consumers of these fabrics, who are not directly concerned in the manufacture of similar articles in this country; and let it be borne in mind that they constitute an overwhelming majority of the people,

* Gibbon's " Decline and Fall," Vol. I., Chap. III.

who, through their agents of various grade, title and function, form the government, shape its policy and make the laws by which we are all governed.

In order to a clearer perception of the principle it is my purpose to illustrate, let us assume that the representatives of the foreign manufacturers of cotton and woollen fabrics used by our people, and the representatives of the American consumers of these fabrics not directly concerned in that class of manufactures—let us suppose they met at our frontier to trade—the foreigners to sell, the Americans to purchase, a year's supply of cotton and woollen goods. Negotiations open by the foreigners, who exhibit their fabrics arranged in parcels marked respectively one dollar, and various multiples of one dollar. The American agents examine the goods attentively and marvel at their excellence, and more especially at their cheapness. Indeed, the low prices excite their alarm, and they decide that the parcels offered for one hundred cents must be raised to one hundred and fifty cents, and the larger parcels in proportion—the excess above the asking price to be paid to the officers of the government of their own forming—in order to protect American industries from the ruinous competition of cheap foreign labor! Having established regulations to that effect and provided means for enforcing them, the representatives of "American labor" not interested in competing manufactures, lay in a stock of cotton and woollen goods for and at the cost of their principals, and they congratulate themselves and their fellow-dupes that they have outwitted the crafty foreign manufacturers who had cunningly adapted their fabrics to the necessities and tastes of the American people, and then offered them here at prices absurdly low, for the special purpose of bringing American labor down to the degraded level of the pauper labor of Europe and thereby ruining American industry!

A REVENUE TARIFF.

The plan of this work, if rigidly adhered to, would perhaps forbid any consideration of a "revenue tariff," as such. Its main object is to point out the conditions of the largest possible production, the elements, forces or factors of production being given; to show that a protective tariff must necessarily produce a change in those conditions as a means of making its influence felt by the industries of the country; and hence that its net effect must be a diminution in the aggregate of values produced. All this, it is assumed, has already been done.

It may be remarked that political economy can

recognize no distinction between a revenue tariff and a protective tariff, except such as may be based on the difference in the scale of duties they respectively impose. In this case names possess no practical significance whatever. A tariff act might be so drawn as to embrace only such articles or commodities as this country does not produce—viz., teas, coffees, spices, etc.; and to such an act the name "revenue tariff" would properly apply. But no tariff of this kind has ever been adopted by any country within my knowledge.

A "revenue tariff," as that term is used in this country, means a scale of duties so adjusted as to produce the greatest possible amount of revenue without regard to its "incidental" effect upon the vocations and industries of the people. But suppose a duty of thirty per cent. on a given commodity should be incorporated in a revenue tariff, because in the opinion of the legislature, such a rate of duty would yield more revenue than a higher or a lower rate—it is obvious it would exert precisely the same effect upon the industries of the country and the occupations of the people, as if it formed a part of a tariff enacted avowedly to protect the American producers of similar commodities against foreign competition. That is, it would benefit the American producer by raising prices, and to the same extent it would injure the consumer. And in so far as it should " diversify industry " by diverting capital and labor from other pursuits to that of producing the protected commodity, it would violate the conditions of the largest possible production, and prove detrimental to the interests of the people in the aggregate. Why and how these results would follow the measures indicated has already been explained.

It must be evident to the reader from what precedes, that the more scrupulously the people observe the natural laws applicable to the matter under consideration, and the more carefully they fulfil the conditions of the largest possible production, the greater will be the rewards of their industry and the better able they will be to bear any given burden of taxation. That civil governments find it practicable by means of duties on imports, to raise a larger sum for public uses, from a smaller annual product and a smaller aggregate of wealth than they could raise by direct taxation from a people of larger income and greater wealth, without exciting more or less serious discontent, is undoubtedly true. This fact furnishes one reason why governments almost universally favor this mode of taxation. But this line of discussion is scarcely pertinent to economical science, and it will be pursued no further.

APPENDIX A.

A PAPER READ BEFORE THE ROCHESTER FREE TRADE LEAGUE.

JANUARY, 1851, BY ISAAC BUTTS.

Question—Supposing all nations to have enacted prohibitory or highly Protective Tariffs, would the aggregate interests of our country be best promoted by similar legislation, or by absolute Free Trade ?

This question, taken in its fullest extent, includes the whole issue between the advocates of Protection and their antagonists. Many ponderous volumes have been written, and many of the best intellects of this age have taken opposite sides upon it, and labored (according to their own estimation, with equal success) to demonstrate the correctness of their irreconcilable theories. It would be presumptuous, then, to assume that the subject is entirely free from difficulties ; or that it can be satisfactorily disposed of in a brief essay, the production of a leisure hour.

Hence, I shall not enter into a minute or detailed argument; but shall simply state, as concisely as I may be able in the little time now at my command, some of the reasons why all attempts to benefit the industry of the Nation as a whole, or to mitigate or to neutralize the effect of unfriendly legislation by other States, by the imposition of Protective or any other duties by our own government, must not only prove abortive, but positively injurious to the interests which it is desired to promote.

In the first instance, in order to ascertain whether the aggregate wealth of a country is increased by the imposition of import duties, we should inquire how wealth is produced;

what elements enter into its composition ; and whether these elements are multiplied by that policy, or their activity, so to speak, increased.

An analysis of the phenomena of production, demonstrates the fact that all wealth is formed by human labor acting upon, or in conjunction with, natural agents ; or, in other words, by means of human labor, assisted by nature herself, working up the "raw material," which nature has furnished in abundance for the free use of every individual of our race. A thorough investigation of the subject leads to the inevitable conclusion, in my opinion, that, philosophically speaking, two elements alone enter into the production of wealth: human Labor and Natural Agents; in which latter must be included the operation of natural forces, as well as the endless variety of material things, of which nature's storehouse furnishes an inexhaustible supply.

Now it seems to me perfectly clear that, in order to increase the ratio of production, it is necessary to multiply the elements that enter into the composition and production of wealth; *or*, to increase the activity of these elements in the work of production.

If I am right in these positions, the whole issue is narrowed down to these simple questions : Does the levying of import duties increase the *quantity* of human laborers, or of the materials or the forces of nature? And does that policy give additional *activity* to these elements.

These questions—if I have chosen the proper language in which to state them—comprise the whole issue. It will not be seriously pretended that Protective duties, or legislation of any kind whatever, can directly increase the quantity of human labor ; nor of Matter ; nor of Natural Forces. To suppose the contrary, would involve the possession by man of the creative power—the endowment of a finite being with the attributes of Omnipotence.

We have but a single inquiry left : would the policy in question give greater *activity* to the elements of wealth? Would it lead to their more active co-operation in the phenomena of production—and, consequently, to an increase of products or of values in the aggregate?

To answer this, we must remember that only *one* of these elements is endowed with intellect, with volition, with a moral nature, with appetites and passions. The other is a mere passive, inanimate, unreasoning agent. Any stimulant calculated to tend to increased activity, must therefore be addressed to that *partner* in the work of production which thinks, feels and wills—to Labor, to Man.

Now the only way to stimulate Labor which the case admits of, is to *increase its reward*.

Reverting to our original hypothesis—that all other nations imposed heavy duties on our products and we none on theirs, would the imposition of countervailing duties increase the reward of Labor? Keeping in view the principles laid down above, this question is easily answered.

Labor is the thinking and the willing element in the process of production; matter and the forces of Nature constitute the passive one. The whole domain or storehouse of Nature is open to Labor from which it may choose its materials or invite her co-operation. It needs no argument to prove that it is always the object of Labor to make Nature bear the largest possible share of the work of production. Illustrations of this fact are innumerable and will press themselves upon the attention of the least reflective. If then other nations had by the imposition of duties interfered with the natural market of some or all of our products, Labor endowed with Intellect would institute an examination into the effect of such Legislation. It would be found that in the production of some articles, Nature is in particular countries far more lavish of her aid than in the production of others. If the invidious legislation of foreign countries had imposed a tax on the importation of a certain article, in the production of which Labor had hitherto secured here its largest reward, which tax should exactly neutralize the superior degree in which nature cooperated in its production, above certain other articles, it would thereafter be a matter of complete indifference whether

Labor continued in its accustomed channel or resorted to the production of the other articles assumed to be placed by the legislation referred to in the same category as regards the profits they would yield to Labor. If such legislation should impose a tax which should not fully neutralize the superior effectiveness of Nature's co-operation in the case assumed, Labor, guided by intellect, would still produce the same articles, because it would thus realize the largest reward. But if the tax should *more* than countervail the more effective co-operation of Nature in producing the articles supposed, Labor would then make an intelligent examination to learn *what article besides* the proscribed one Nature would assist most in producing. And having found the article in the production of which, under all the circumstances, Nature would be most liberal in her favors and thus secure to human Industry the largest net reward, Labor would enter in this new field, and thus Free Trade would leave the matter so far as we are concerned conscious that the legislation of other Nations affected injuriously the Industry of our People ; but that all attempts to compensate for these injuries by '' Protective '' duties levied on goods consumed by ourselves would simply aggravate the evils for which they are urged as a remedy.

But, to continue our last hypothesis, that other nations imposed duties on some or all of our products, while we admitted all theirs free, and that labor here, guided by intelligence, had sought such employment as under all the circumstances secured most of Nature's aid and yielded the largest net profit—let us see in what way—a tax on imports, i. e., Protective duties, would operate.

All the labor of the countries in the case supposed is employed in such vocations as nature indicates ; i. e., every man is engaged in producing such articles as, in his opinion pay him best.

Why THEY pay him best we have already explained, and it is unnecessary to recapitulate. It is clear that in reference to the articles *not* produced nature does *not*, in the opinion of the producers, bestow her aid so lavishly as she does in the production of those which engage their efforts. And in order to make the production of articles *not* now produced, more lucrative than that of those which *are* produced, we must do to our own people precisely what we regarded as hostile and unjust in other nations: we must drive labor from the production of articles where nature is MORE, to others where she is LESS lavish of her co-operation. This is done by imposing duties on articles of this better class ; so that the taxes paid (in the shape of duties) by the producers of the former, more than countervails the advantages they derive from the superior co-operation of nature. A portion or all the labor engaged in producing the former articles, is driven to abandon the business and it seeks other employment less favored by nature indeed ; but also less persecuted by man.

The net loss to the community and to the world occasioned by this policy is precisely the difference between the value of the products which a given amount of labor would produce in a business which it had sought in the absence of all duties or artificial regulation ; and the value of the products which the same labor would produce in the business to which it had been driven by such duties or artificial regulation—the value of the products in the latter case to be ascertained by applying to them the price which prevailed prior to the adoption of protective duties (if recent); or rather, to be more philosophic, by taking the price of such products which wou'd have *then* obtained in the absence of such duties or artificial regulation. It is clear that the loss in this case is precisely the difference in the practical effective energy of nature, which labor would call into requisition in the respective hypotheses. In the absence of artificial regulation, labor seeks such partnerships with nature as develop the largest possible share of the work of production upon the latter. But when driven from such associations by the insidious operation of protective tariffs, labor still seeks such other associations with its old partner as will yield the largest net return for the same quantity of its only commodity after taking into account all the circumstances which affect the measure of value in the resulting product.

APPENDIX B.

"Mais ces forces naturelles, considérées en elles-mêmes, et abstraction faite de tout travail intellectuel ou musculaire, sont des dons *gratuits* de la Providence ; et à ce titre, elles restent sans *valeur* à travers toutes les complications des transactions humaines. C'est la pensée dominante de cet écrit." [*Œuvres Complètes de Frédéric Bastiat;* Vol. VI., p. 83,]

" * * * Nous avons cherché partout la Valeur, nous l'avons constatée partout où elle existe, c'est-à-dire, partout où il y a *échange de services;* nous l'avons trouvée partout identique à elle-même, fondée sur un principe clair, simple, absolu, quoique influencée par une multitude de circonstances diverses. Nous aurions passé en revue tous nos autres besoins, * * * que nous n'aurions jamais trouvé autre chose : souvent de la matière, quelquefois des forces fournies *gratuitement* par la nature, toujours des services humains s'échangeant entre eux, se mesurant, s'estimant, s'appréciant, s'*evaluant* les uns par les autres. et manifestant seuls le résultat de cette évaluation ou la VALEUR." *Ib.* 166,

" En effet, si la valeur est dans la matière, elle se confond avec les qualités physiques des corps qui les rendent utiles à l'homme. Or ces qualités y sont souvent mises par la nature. Donc la nature concourt à créer la *valeur*, et nous voilà attribuant de la Valeur à ce qui est *gratuit et commun* par essence. Où est donc alors la base de la *propriété?* Quand la rémunération que je cède pour acquérir un produit matériel, du blé, par exemple, se distribue entre tous les travailleurs qui, à l'occasion de ce produit, m'ont, de près ou de loin, rendu quelque *service*, à qui va cette part de rémunération correspondante à la portion de *Valeur* due à la nature étrangère à l'homme? Va-t-elle à Dieu? Nul ne le soutient, et l'on n'a jamais vu Dieu réclamer son salaire. Va-t-elle à un homme? A quel titre, puisque, dans l'hypothèse, il na rien fait?"—[*Ib.* p. 171.

Il est donc exact de dire qu'au point de vue personnel, l'homme, par le travail, devient propriétaire de l'utilité naturelle (il ne travaille que pour cela), quelque soit le rapport, variable à l'infini, du travail à l'utilité. Mais au point de vue *social*, à l'égard les uns des autres, les hommes ne sont jamais propriétaires que de la valeur, laquelle n'a pas pour fondement la libéralité de la nature, mais le service humain, la peine prise, le danger couru, l'habilité déployée pour recueillir cette libéralité ; en un mot, en ce qui concerne l'utilité naturelle et gratuite, le dernier acquéreur, celui à qui doit aboutir la satisfaction, est mis, par l'échange, exactment au lieu et place du premier travailleur"--*Ib.* p. 267.

" Et si la richesse *sociale, acquise,créée,* de *valeur, onéreuse,* en un mot la Propriété, est inégalement répartie, on ne peut pas dire qu'elle le soit injustement, puisqu'elle est pour chacun proportionelle aux *services* d'où elle procède et dont elle n'est que l'évaluation."—*Ib.* p. 287.

"Mais les forces et les matériaux, donnés par Dieu gratuitement à l'homme dès l'origine, sont demeurés, sont encore et seront toujours gratuits, à travers toutes les transactions humaines ; car, dans les appréciations auxquelles donnent lieu les échanges, ce sont les *services humains*, et non les *dons de Dieu* qui *s'évaluent.*"—*Ib.* p. 297.

" Si j'y parviens, si je démontre que les agents naturels, même appropriés, ne produisent pas de la Valeur, mais de l'Utilité qui, passant par la main du propriétaire, sans y rien laisser, arrive gratuitement au consommateur," etc.—*Ib.* p. 308.

" L'homme, sous l'influence de l'intérêt personnel, recherche toujours, et nécessairement, les circonstances qui peuvent donner le plus de *valeur* à ses services. Il ne tarde pas à reconnaitre, qu'à l'égard des dons de Dieu, il peut être favorisé de trois manières :

1. Où s'il s'empare seul de ces dons eux-mêmes :
2. Où s'il connait seul le *procédé* par lequel il est possible de les utiliser :
3. Où s'il possède seul l'instrument au moyen duquel on peut les faire concourir.

Dans l'une ou l'autre de ces circonstances, il donne *peu* de son travail contre *beaucoup* de travail d'autrui. Ses services ont une grande *valeur* relative et l'on est disposé à croire que cet excédent de valeur est inhérent à l'agent naturel."—*Ib.* p. 356.

THE END.

www.ingramcontent.com/pod-product-compliance
Lightning Source LLC
Chambersburg PA
CBHW020242170426
43202CB00008B/188